COLD-WEATHER CAMPING

Ray Stebbins

Henry Regnery Company · Chicago

Library of Congress Cataloging in Publication Data

Stebbins, Ray.
    Cold-weather camping.

    Includes index.
    1. Snow camping.   I. Title.
GV198.9.S83   1975   796.54   75-12864
ISBN 0-8092-8223-2
ISBN 0-8092-8222-4 pbk.

Published by Henry Regnery Company
         180 North Michigan Avenue
         Chicago, Illinois 60601
Manufactured in the United States of America
Library of Congress Catalog Card Number: 75-12864
International Standard Book Number: 0-8092-8223-2 (cloth)
                       0-8092-8222-4 (paper)

Published simultaneously in Canada by
Beaverbooks
953 Dillingham Road
Pickering, Ontario L1W 1Z7
Canada

Contents

To my mother

Acknowledgments

Few books could be written without the help of friends who give of their knowledge and that most valuable possession, their time. I am indebted to Dr. John Gosar, famous guide and tracker, for the F.A.A.B. award, which gave me the confidence to undertake this book, and for his untiring instructions on the ways of the woods and the cards; to his brother, Jack Gosar, outdoorsman, for sharing his knowledge and enjoyment of the back country, and his sourmash; to Bill Brimmer, expert on snow and survival, for his uncomplaining help on winter ventures; to Norman Weis, photographer, writer and expert packer, for his encouragement and advice; to David Sumner, writer, outdoorsman and mentor, for his tutelage and timely prodding. I am especially indebted to my wife for her patience and help. Were it not for her, this book would have been written in longhand.

Introduction

Back in the early 1800s, mountain man John Colter made one of the most remarkable winter trips ever recorded in the annals of the North American wilderness. Even for a pioneer, Colter had more than his share of adventurous spirit. While his comrades huddled about their cabin fires at Lisa's Fort, John challenged the snowy wilderness of the Rockies. Carrying only a thirty-pound backpack, he traveled on foot through more than 500 miles of rugged mountain country in the dead of winter.

Today, a growing number of Americans and Canadians are discovering that they are closer in spirit to Colter than to his companions who stayed by the fire. It is for these new mountain men at heart that this book was written. I have tried to make it a practical book. With a few obvious exceptions (such as $30,000 motor homes) the equipment and techniques described have actually been used by my friends and me in the winter wilderness. You will find, I trust, more than enough information to enable you to enjoy cold-weather camping.

This book has been written to encourage you to share in something that I have truly enjoyed, for cold-weather camping is a recreational activity and should be fun. Yet it is more than mere recreation. It's good for your nerves, your health, and your pride, for there is considerable satisfaction in this ultimate camping experience.

It is an activity open to everyone, which makes it an ideal outdoor venture for families to share. There are no requirements of age or toughness. Today, even babies are packed into the snowy back country. Sharing the adventure and excitement of winter camping can be a powerful, uniting experience. It may not close the generation gap, but it can help bridge it.

Cold-weather camping also can be an inner adventure. It is an intimate way of knowing the winter world and its wonders. In finding a deeper appreciation of its beauty, you will grow. You will find basic perspectives coming into sharper focus when your major concerns are elemental — for food, shelter, and warmth. New insights can well expand the outer limits of your own sufficiency.

It is also a new way of sharing the world, for it will put you inside the skin of primitive man. You will know with deep intensity his feelings toward the sun, the wind, and the snow. With him, you will worship sun and fire, and you will know with atavistic certainty why the North Wind is evil and the West Wind is good.

You also will share the adventurous spirit of Colter, and come to know that joyous feeling of independence that has always drawn North Americans to the far and difficult places.

Winter campsite at Shoshone Pass in Wyoming's newly created Washakie Wilderness. (Photo by Ray Stebbins)

1

What to Take

Basic Equipment

Choosing the right equipment for cold-weather camping is crucial to safe enjoyment of the sport. Yet there is no mystery about it. There is a wide variety of gear available in every price range, and comparing the relative merits of items and deciding which suits your individual needs is part of the fun. If you are a summer camper, you'll already have some of the necessary things and may have to make only a few additional purchases. Starting from scratch, your investment could run up to several hundred dollars. Even so, your outlay will be less than is required to get started in many sports. After the initial investment, the expenses of winter camping are relatively low.

Initial costs will be determined by the kind of camping you intend to do. Basically there are two types of winter campers — those who prefer operating out of a comfortable base camp and those who would rather backpack and live in the snow. Though much of the equipment is the same for both groups, requirements for packs, sleeping bags, and tents are different.

On the left is a standard contour pack frame and on the right, a frame from the army version of the Bergans-Meis rucksack skiing pack. (Photo by Ray Stebbins)

PACKS

A backpacker's choice of pack will depend on the method he uses to travel in snow. Cross-country skiers need a pack that carries the weight low, while snowshoers can use a standard, framed backpack that holds the weight of the load as high as possible.

Skiers' Backpacks

The Bergans-Meis pack and its variations were once the favorites of skiers. They consist of a large, alpine rucksack

Touring pack with built-in frame features padded waistband and removable outside pockets. (Photo courtesy of Milt McLaskey and Dana Van Burgh)

mounted on a light A-frame. A band of webbing across the bottom of the frame holds the carrier away from the packer's back, and the top of the A-frame rests between the shoulders on a pad. Some are equipped with a belt, which helps somewhat in transferring part of the pack weight from the shoulders to the hips. The army version, used by our ski troops and once popular due to its availability as a surplus item, has a heavy canvas sack with three outside pockets. It can still be found in a few discount stores. Although heavier and less convenient than more modern designs, it has the advantages of being very rugged and inexpensive.

Skier with standard contour pack. This pack is popular with summer campers and is a good pack for snowshoers to carry, too. (Photo courtesy of Milt McLasky and Dana Van Burgh)

Newer versions of the skier's backpack are called touring or mountaineering packs. They represent a considerable improvement over the older styles. They consist of a nylon rucksack, usually waterproofed, which is carried by shoulder straps attached directly to the bag. Most of these packs are stiffened by aluminum stays that lie against the packer's back and that can be bent to fit body contour. Most are provided with three outside pockets and a map pouch, as well as tabs and straps to hold your skis. (The last item is a handy one when you have to hike several miles to reach the snow.) I'd want all of these features on my touring pack. The real advantage of the touring design is in keeping pack weight down toward the small of the back. This lowers the skier's center of gravity, giving him better control. Also, the pack is frameless and rides tight against the back, which helps control by reducing the pendulum effect common to all frame-type packs.

If you already have a standard, contour frame backpack,

This skier is carrying the army version of the Bergans-Meis ski pack. This is a better choice for the skier since it enables him to carry the heavy part of the load low on his back. (Photo by Ray Stebbins)

you can still use it even though you plan to travel on skis. Load the heaviest items in the bottom of the pack and cinch up your waist band tightly. It won't be as easy to use as the touring pack, but if you're a polished skier, you can handle it.

Snowshoers' Backpacks

The camper who chooses snowshoes will want the same, top-heavy type gear that the summer camper uses. The most popular backpack, by far, is the contour frame with matching nylon bag. The ladderlike frame is made of aluminum tubing with bracing of aluminum rod. Contoured to the body, it curves in slightly over the shoulders and flares out over the hips. The frame is held away from the packer's back by one or two wide nylon bands that also protect him from hard objects in the load. The bands should have some easy adjustment to keep them taut.

Proper size of the contour frame is determined by the packer's height. The frame should be long enough so that the top is about level with the top of the head and the belt is at the hip, just below the top of the hip bone (it should never go around the waist). A frame fifteen inches wide and twenty-nine to thirty inches long will fit the average camper. Adjustable frames are available, but the added weight and higher cost make them less appealing.

The harness is attached to the frame and consists of padded shoulder straps and belt. The straps should be adjustable for width where they attach to the upper frame and the belt should be equipped with a quick-release buckle.

For the packsack, it's a good idea to stay with the heavier nylon in the six-to eight-ounce range. Avoid the light, taffeta nylon used in the cheaper imports. The interior stitching and finish of the bag are the best clues to quality. In general, a bag fifteen inches across by nine inches deep by twenty-two inches long is large enough for most winter camping. Along with the outside pockets, this will give you enough load space to easily handle a week's trip in winter.

Some packsacks consist of one large bag. A better arrangement is one that is divided into two main sections, each with its own access. This setup makes it easy to distribute weight properly. The upper portion should be larger; it will take the heavier, bulkier items. How to load the pack is discussed in Chapter 3. There should be at least four outside pockets — five is better. Like the divided bag, the pockets provide for easy weight and balance adjustments and add convenience by making it possible to reach often-used items without disturbing the whole load.

Recently, a different type of frame has been selling well on the West Coast. It is variously called the hip-hugger, hip-carry, or wrap-around frame. This design has an extension that curves halfway around the packer's waist. The extension consists of aluminum outrigger arms or aluminum reinforcement of the heavily padded waist band and is attached to the frame by swivels. The frame itself is usually straighter than the contour model. The idea of the design is to move the point of carry — or center of the weight load — forward, in line with the hip bones, and to place nearly all of the load directly on the hips.

The wrap-around frame is supposed to carry more weight more comfortably than the contour model. The design, however, has some serious drawbacks. It must be fitted to the packer by someone who knows the product. Packers who are slim or plump cannot be fitted. If you are tall or short, a more costly adjustable type is required. In addition, the hip-carry frame is heavier, bulkier, and more expensive than the standard contour design. Such considerations make the hip-hugger a poor choice for the beginning packer and, in fact, probably a poor choice for most of us.

I recommend the contour frame and matching bag for the snowshoer and the touring model (with aluminum stays) for the skier. Either pack should have a minimum capacity of 3,000 cubic inches. This size backpack will hold thirty to forty pounds, enough to keep you in the wilderness for a week or more. The packsacks should be of eight-ounce Urethane-

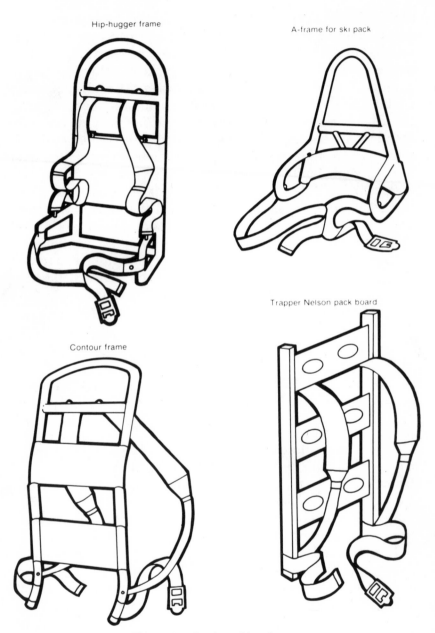

Hip-hugger frame

A-frame for ski pack

Contour frame

Trapper Nelson pack board

Figure 1.   Backpacking frames

coated nylon and I'd want three outside pockets on the touring model and five on the contour sack. In either style, the total weight shouldn't be quite sixty ounces. I'd be sticky about that.

There are still a few packs in both models that don't have a hip belt. Never buy a pack without one. Experienced campers can tell you that carrying a pack without a belt is as tiresome as chopping wood with a rubber ax. Also, don't buy one of the cheap, discounted imports. A good pack is expensive, but quality is important. The pack takes heavy abuse on the trail and an inferior product won't stand up. So, if you're in the market for a pack, buy a good one. Should it turn out that you don't like cold-weather camping, a top quality product has good resale value; junk doesn't.

Day Packs

Even the camper who operates out of a base camp will need a pack for his daily trips. All he requires, however, is a small, frameless day pack. This is merely a pear-shaped nylon sack fitted with shoulder straps and a belt (this style does go around the waist). I'd pick one that has two or three outside pockets and a capacity of about 1200 cubic inches. In it, you can carry extra clothing, a warm jacket, lunch, energy foods, a small survival kit, wet gear, and perhaps a camera or some fishing equipment. There are plenty of these small packs available at reasonable prices. They are handy for the camper to have any time of the year.

BEDDING

In addition to his pack, the camper who goes out to live in the snow will need a high quality sleeping bag. Nothing can spoil your taste for winter camping any quicker than a tense, wakeful night in a cold sack. So, it's worth some time and effort to select the proper gear. Among winter campers, and among backpackers in general, the most popular type of sleeping bag is made of prime goose down.

Down Bags

If you consult almost any backpacking supplier's catalog, you'll find an impassioned and lengthy plug for the quality of the down he uses in his equipment. Unfortunately, there really is a difference, and prime quality goose down is expensive. If you buy a down bag for winter camping, it will be the most costly item of your equipment, with the possible exception of your tent. Yet down remains the best choice for ease in packing and comfort in sleeping.

In order to conserve weight and bulk, down bags carried by packers are slim-lined. The narrowest models are described as mummy bags. The slightly wider models are called modified mummy or barrel shape. The mummy bag fits closely around the body. When you move, so does the bag. Most campers prefer the larger, modified versions. Wider at shoulders and hips and with more foot room, these bags do permit some body movement. My feeling is that the extra cost and slight extra weight are worth it. But the choice is a matter of personal taste.

In choosing your bag, you'll want to take into consideration your height. Most down bags are classed as regular or large. The regular size is supposed to fit campers up to six feet tall. If, however, you are five foot ten or more, go for the larger model.

Basically, a down sleeping bag is made of two nylon shells, one inside the other, with a fill between them of several pounds of down. Nylon (generally about two-ounce weight) is used for the shells because it is tough and windproof, yet porous enough to permit the down to "breathe," carrying body moisture out of the bag. For this reason, the nylon is never waterproofed. In quality bags, the inner shell is cut in a smaller diameter than the outer shell. Most manufacturers call this a "differential" cut. The purpose is to permit the down to loft or fluff more completely. Within limits, the more the down lofts or expands, the more efficient an insulator it becomes. In addition, this design reduces cold spots since elbows and knees can't compress the down as easily as in the full-cut models. This is definitely a feature you will want in a

This modified mummy bag by Adventure Pack, Inc., features slant box construction, differential cut, and differential fill with three-fourths of the down in the top section. A standard bag weighs three pounds seven ounces. This is an excellent winter bag. (Photo courtesy of Adventure Pack, Inc.)

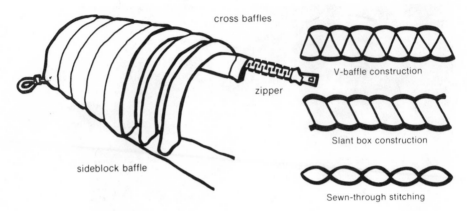

cross baffles

V-baffle construction

zipper

Slant box construction

sideblock baffle

Sewn-through stitching

Figure 2.   Sleeping bag construction

winter sleeping bag. Another mark of quality bags is that the down is kept in place by a series of internal nylon baffles. Light liners and some of the less expensive summer down bags have sewn-through stitching. In this case, the two nylon shells are sewn to each other with a number of horizontal and vertical seams. These seams form a series of square or rectangular pockets that hold the down in place. Since the stitching goes through both layers of nylon at the same point, a series of tiny holes is formed along the seams. Cold air, of course, leaks through the holes. Obviously this is not an acceptable design for winter use. In selecting a down bag for cold-weather use, make certain that the internal strips of cloth or baffles that hold the shells together and form channels or tubes to keep the down in place are slanted and parallel or in a V design. This assures that the upper and lower seams of the shells will not be in line and thus no cold spots can develop along the stitching.

There are, of course, less important details of design to consider. The majority of quality backpacking bags today are made with a built-in hood that can be tightened around the camper's face with a drawstring. Some models, however, provide a detachable hood. I recommend the built-in type because it eliminates the possibility of cold drafts leaking in where the hood attaches to the bag. In any case, the hood is a good idea; it increases the warmth of your sleeping bag measurably.

Some manufacturers offer a design with a differential fill. This means that they put more down in the top of the bag than in the bottom section. The usual ratio is about 60/40. The theory is that since the underside of the bag will be insulated by a foam plastic mattress pad, it won't require as much down as the top side, which is exposed to the cold air. The idea makes good sense. However, you would need a type large enough to allow you to turn over without moving the bag. The mummy style, of course, is not suitable for differential fill. Other items, such as zipper length and minor details of construction, have little to do with the warming efficiency of the bag.

The most important part of selecting sleeping gear is in choosing a bag with the right comfort range. To help you, manufacturers provide a minimum comfort rating for their product, that is, the minimum cold temperature at which the sleeping bag will keep the "average" camper warm. Since no one is "average" the figure given is merely an estimate and should be used only as a guide.

The minimum comfort rating of a bag is not determined by its total weight. It is the weight of the down fill, coupled with the design of the bag, that determines how warm it will be.

In a regular size, well designed and constructed mummy bag, two pounds of prime goose down fill will keep the average camper warm in temperatures down to about -5 degrees F. In the modified or barrel types, quality and construction being the same, it will take about two and a quarter pounds to provide the same warmth. Two and a half pounds in a mummy bag, or two and three-quarter pounds in the larger model, will take the comfort range down to around -20 degrees F. It will require some three pounds of fill to push the figure down to -30 degrees F. Remember, however, the figures apply only to bags of top quality construction, filled with prime grade, white goose down. A list of suppliers who furnish such equipment will be found in the appendix.

Often the tendency among backpackers is to choose

sleeping gear that is too warm. Such a bag can be just as uncomfortable as one that is too cold. Choice of a winter sleeping bag will depend on how warmly you sleep, the type of tent used and the average temperatures you expect to encounter. Past experience is the best guide, but in general terms, most cold-weather campers will find that a bag with a minimum range of -20 degrees F. will handle most winter situations. On those very cold nights when temperatures drop into the -40s, some extra clothing worn to bed will provide the necessary additional warmth. This weight bag can also be used nicely in spring and fall.

On the other hand, if you will be camping in a well designed tent and in areas where the temperatures are seldom much below freezing, you may be more comfortable in a lighter bag in the zero to -5 degree range.

If you already have a good down bag for summer, it can be used in combination with another for use in winter. As an example, I often take a light liner with one pound of goose down fill to put inside a heavier bag with two pounds of fill. It makes a warm combination, though it is slightly bulkier than a single bag. It does, however, give me two bags for warmer weather rather than one bag suitable only for winter.

Prime' goose down is not the only choice available to the cold-weather camper. There is at least one other material that is suitable for winter use.

Dacron Fiberfill II

The E. I. du Pont Company, manufacturers of Dacron 88, are now producing a second generation polyester fiber, which they call Dacron Fiberfill II. When used in sleeping bags, its characteristics resemble those of prime goose down. Furthermore, it offers some important advantages over down.

First of these is price. Presently, a good quality bag of Fiberfill II sells for half the price, or less, of a good down sack. Unlike down, it is hand or machine washable and can be machine dried. Since it absorbs only one percent moisture, it dries very quickly. It also keeps its shape when wet and does not mat or lump like down. This means that even when soaked, it will retain at least some of its insulating qualities.

On the other hand, while it resembles down in certain respects, it isn't an exact copy. It is only ninety percent as compressible as goose down. In actual use, I've found that it makes a bulky load on the packframe. Moreover, it has less insulating ability. It takes nearly one and a half pounds of Dacron Fiberfill II to equal one pound of quality goose down. Construction and fabrics being the same, it would require a bag containing three and a half pounds of Fiberfill II to equal one or two and a half pounds down. Since winter pack loads tend to be heavy, this added weight could be a real disadvantage. Also, Fiberfill II lacks the coziness and comfort of down.

Yet, all things considered, the new Dacron makes an excellent choice for the cold-weather camper on a budget, or for use in areas where you encounter wet conditions as well as cold.

Whatever bag you choose, stay with quality. It may cost more initially, but its superior warmth and wearing ability will make it a bargain. Most down sleeping bags are stuffed (never compressed by rolling) in a sack that is water repellent. If yours doesn't have such a sack, it's worth the extra cost to buy one of treated nylon.

Mattress Pads

In addition to the sleeping bag, you will need a foam plastic mattress pad. It is necessary not only to give you a soft sleeping surface, but also to insulate your bag against the cold ground or snow. There are two types used by most packers: Ensolite pads in thicknesses up to one-half inch and polyurethane foam pads that run one and a half to two inches in thickness.

Ensolite pads, sometimes called "closed-cell foam," will not absorb water and need no waterproof covering. In half-inch thickness, Ensolite's insulating qualities are effective to about

-10 degrees F. It is less bulky, less expensive and lighter than urethane. However, it is difficult to find a single-width piece longer than fifty-six inches. This is barely long enough to allow a short camper to stretch out. Moreover, at temperatures much below -40 degrees, Ensolite tends to harden and crack like an eggshell.

On the other hand, the urethane or open-cell foam pads will soak up water like a sponge, so they must be covered with waterproof nylon, which adds to cost and weight. In a two-inch thickness, however, it makes far more comfortable sleeping, especially on hard-frozen ground. In addition, it will retain its insulating qualities in severe cold and can be purchased in longer lengths.

Perhaps the best available pad is a new product from Eastern Mountain Sports. It is called Volarafoam. A closed-cell foam, it is lighter and less expensive than Ensolite. It also has better insulating qualities and will retain its flexibility at -50 degrees F. A piece 9/16 inches thick and twenty-five by sixty inches will weigh only a pound. Its one drawback is that abrasion resistance is not as great as that of other foam pads. Nevertheless, it is the preferred material for winter camping.

In any case, avoid air mattresses. Besides being cumbersome and uncomfortable, they lack the insulating qualities so necessary in a cold-weather sleeping pad.

Once you have purchased a good backpack and quality sleeping gear, there is only one other item of basic equipment that will require any real outlay of cash. That, is a shelter.

TENTS

In recent years, the number of tents specially designed for backpacking has mushroomed into a fantastic array of styles in an equally wide range of prices. Unfortunately, nearly all of these tents are designed for summer. There are expedition tents, but they generally are too heavy and too expensive for recreation purposes. Nevertheless, it is easy to point out the characteristics that make a good winter tent.

First of all, it must be stable enough to handle the high winds that often accompany winter storms. Stability is a function of design. Basically, it involves the suspension system, the poles and guy lines that support the tent, and the catenary cut, which means shaping the walls to conform with the natural sag of the ridge line. The idea is to produce a tent whose walls are drum tight and wrinkle free. A taut tent, suspension being the same, is more stable than a loose one. Tautness also reduces wind flap. Anyone who has spent a night listening to the drumroll flapping of tent walls can appreciate this feature.

There are three types of suspension used for most backpacking tents. The simple I-pole is generally used in the less-expensive summer models. It consists of two single poles set in line with the ridge, at the front and back of the tent. It requires three guy lines to hold each pole. This suspension is less stable than the other types and, in addition, the front pole blocks the entrance, making it less convenient.

A summer pack tent with simple I-pole construction (in this case a ski pole) was used by the author for several winters but is not recommended. (Photo by Ray Stebbins)

This A-frame mountaineering tent with tunnel entrance is excellent for winter use but rather heavy. (Photo courtesy of Page Fagan)

By far the most popular system is the A-frame. In this case, two poles run down the leading and back edges of the walls to the corners, forming a barless A at the front and rear of the tent. Usually, the poles fit through sleeves sewn along the tent edges. Only one guy line is required, since the A-frame is self-supporting in its own plane. This is a very stable arrangement and makes for a tight tent when walls are properly designed.

The third group includes the dome and semi-circular tents. Their support system is a rather complex combination of aluminum or fiberglass poles that fit together in various curved designs. They resemble either an igloo or a quonset hut. The wind shedding qualities of curved surfaces make them quite stable. In high winds, however, they often flex violently.

This dome-type tent is stable and roomy but weighs in at eight pounds. (Photo courtesy of Milt McLaskey and Dana Van Burgh)

This places a severe strain on the poles and failure of pole joints is not uncommon in some models. Yet the shapes of these tents require less material than others that have the same interior space. As a result, the dome and quonset tents are lighter than other styles. They also are warmer because there is less heat loss from their smaller surface areas.

Stability is important, so I'd try to confine my choice to the A-frame or quonset style. A-frames are more readily available and usually less expensive.

Sufficient interior space is another requirement of a good winter tent. There should be enough space to shelter both you and your gear. There must also be enough head room to allow you to sit up comfortably, at least in the front of the tent, since much of your cooking and eating may be done inside. For the same reason, a cooking flap, though not essential, is a handy feature. This is a snap-closed or zipper flap in the bottom of the tent, near the front entrance. When opened, it permits you to set your stove or hot pots directly on the ground.

Backpacking tents come in one, two, and three-man sizes. The most popular and practical is the two-man model. The one-man tent is often too small, even for the individual camper, and the three-man job is too crowded and too heavy for packing. The two-man tents are generally about four and a half to five feet at the widest point (to save weight, nearly all backpacking tents taper to the rear). They average about seven to seven and a half feet in length. For a winter tent — as long as weight isn't excessive and quality is retained — the larger the better.

A good ventilation system also is a necessity. The average camper, even in winter, will void a pint of body moisture during the night by perspiring and breathing. If this moisture isn't expelled from the tent, it condenses on the roof and walls. In winter, it often forms ice crystals that melt at the touch or shower you with icy wetness every time you brush the walls of the tent. As soon as you start cooking inside, the crystals melt and drip down on you and your equipment. This unpleasant condensation is difficult to avoid and almost impossible to eliminate.

Most backpacking tents use a porous nylon for the roof and walls. This material allows the moisture to pass through. In order to make the tent waterproof, it must be covered by a treated nylon fly. Such a fly should be of generous proportions and reasonably easy to attach. These tents also have some type of vent system, usually involving a small mesh-covered opening at the front and back.

Double-wall tents generally have a light, untreated nylon inner lining and an outer wall and roof of waterproof nylon. When the tent is properly pitched, there is an air space between the two walls. The air space serves as an insulator as well as allowing some of the moisture to escape and condense on the outer wall. These tents also have a vent system. In practice, I've found that the tent with a fly seems to have fewer problems with condensation than the double-wall tent, especially if there are several inches of space between the fly and the tent. However, the double-wall tent, because of its better insulation, is a very popular winter model.

A few tents use waterproofed nylon throughout and rely entirely on a system of ventilation. Since they do not handle condensation very well, and because wetness is a more serious problem in cold weather, it is best to avoid this type of shelter for winter use.

The tunnel entrance is usually found only on the heavier expedition tents, but it is offered on a few of the light backpacking models. It has some advantage for the winter camper. A zipper can jam, but the simple string closure of the tunnel door is almost impossible to foul up. It's a feature I like but wouldn't insist on.

The same is true of the vestibule. It's handy but not essential. It is merely an extension of the tent wall to form a wind shelter or vestibule around the door. It serves as a place to prepare meals, to eat, and to stash gear out of the weather. It can increase the useful area of a smaller tent.

It would be nice to recommend a light, reasonably priced tent with all of the desirable features mentioned. I doubt that it exists. This means that there will have to be some compromises. I'd hold out for stability, roominess, and light weight and give up some of the rest. In fact, if you have a good summer tent that incorporates those three qualities, it may be adequate for winter use. In view of the cost of a quality backpacking tent, it's worth trying before you invest in a new one.

For several years I did all of my winter camping in a simple I-pole, army-style pack tent. It frosted badly and sagged down in my face under the lightest snow load. Yet if I was careful to pitch it out of the wind, it did a passable job.

My present tent, though a considerable improvement over

Author's present tent is a Stephenson's Warmlite, model 6. It is very stable and roomy, and its double walls make it a warm tent. However, its best feature is weight — less than three and a half pounds. (Photo by Ray Stebbins)

others I've tried, is not ideal. Called a Warmlite Model 6, it is made by Stephenson's. Its unique design features double walls of coated nylon and semi-circular aluminum poles at front and rear. It requires no guy ropes and its prairie schooner shape makes it extremely stable in high winds. One of its best features is space — five feet at the widest point by a generous eleven feet in length. There is plenty of room for two men and all of their gear. Even better is the weight. The tent, complete with pegs and poles, hits the scales at less than three and a half pounds.

It does have some drawbacks. Probably because of the coated-nylon inner lining, it doesn't handle moisture very well. It requires very careful handling when setting up or tearing down. And, in my opinion, it is definitely overpriced. Otherwise, it makes an excellent, year-round shelter.

If you are in the market for a tent, do some careful shopping.

Write to the manufacturers for catalogs (see appendix) and do some comparing. When you have it narrowed down to several choices, write the companies and ask for the names of people who have used their tents. Then write to the buyers and ask about performance. Borrow some tents, if possible. Talk to other campers and to salesmen who have actually had some experience.

Remember that while a good winter tent is expensive, it can be used equally well in summer. The reverse is not always true.

Clothing and Other Essentials

A suitable pack, a warm sleeping bag, and a good tent complete your basic equipment and take care of your major expenses. The rest of your gear won't hurt the budget, especially if you are a summer camper.

CLOTHING

Dressing appropriately for the weather is always important and never more so than in winter. And, if you happen to be impressed by the catalog photos of campers in puffy down parkas, you may envision a large outlay of cash for such clothing, but that isn't necessary.

Wool vs. Down

Heavy down jackets are for mountaineers, not campers; wool is a better choice in most cases. Admittedly, down clothing has far better insulating qualities than wool. It is also much lighter and certainly more compressible. In fact, it is too good. If you wear a heavy down coat, you won't want to wear much else. It will keep you warm if you are merely standing around camp. Yet, most of the time, winter campers are active, and the moment you begin to ski, snowshoe, hike, or even set up a tent, chances are you'll be too warm. Take off the jacket and you're too cold. In short, a heavy down coat is often too much and its warmth is almost impossible to regulate.

Worse, down is useless when wet and it can only be dried slowly and with difficulty. Down clothing is not waterproofed, for in order to retain its insulating qualities, down must breathe to void body moisture. Thus, if you cover your down jacket with wet gear or even a windproof parka, it will soon be soaked by perspiration. If you don't cover the jacket, it can easily get wet from the snow. So, if you rely on a heavy down coat for most of your warmth and it gets wet, you're in real trouble.

Wool, on the other hand, can be worn in layers. In order to adjust body heat, you can peel off or put on just enough to suit your level of activity. Most experienced winter campers wear layers of wool, not because it is less expensive, but because they know how important it is to prevent excessive sweating. Perspiring heavily in winter is dangerous, for it promotes chilling and dehydration. Moreover, wool is the only clothing material that retains some of its warmth, even when wet. For this reason alone, it is better than down for winter wear.

Campers who insist on wearing down should stay with the lighter items, such as vests or shirts. Since these are thin, they can be used as part of the layer system. No one who has spent much time in a winter camp wears a single, heavy coat of any kind. It is not only uncomfortable, but potentially dangerous as well.

Dressing

The winter camper dresses from the skin out for the cold. Probably the ideal underwear is wool longjohns. But most of us don't like wool next to the hide, so we start with a pair of open net underwear and, over that, a pair of waffle-weave or double thick cotton longjohns. The net is an excellent insulator and also keeps the cotton longjohns from taking up body moisture. In cold weather, you want to stay dry both inside and out.

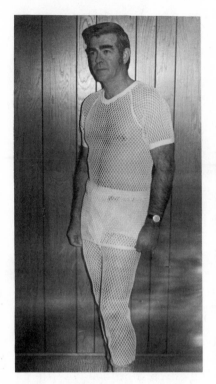

Winter campers should dress for the cold from the skin out, beginning with open net underwear

. . . followed by a double-layered pair of cotton longjohns

Over the underwear goes a regular weight wool shirt and wool pants, which should be a hard-finished worsted. This material sheds wind better than the soft wools and its hard surface won't pick up snow as easily. An extra wool shirt will go in the pack.

Over the shirt, on cold days, I wear the tops of a pair of quilted underwear. (If you prefer, this is the place for a down shirt.) On top of this goes a shirt-jacket of blanket weight wool. For wind protection there is a treated nylon parka with attached hood. It isn't waterproof and shouldn't be. If you are

. . . over which goes an insulated, quilted underwear top (shown) or down shirt

. . . a wool shirt and wool pants

. . . topped finally by a jacket-weight wool shirt, a wool stocking cap that pulls down into a face mask, and heavy mittens called "choppers." (Photos by Ray Stebbins)

packing over rough terrain in a waterproof parka, you're likely to drown in your own sweat. Unless, of course, you remove several layers and pace yourself carefully.

Socks are heavy rag-wool, worn singly with felt liners or two pair at a time with leather ski boots. At least two extra pair of socks go in the pack and, if pack weight isn't running heavy, I'll often add a third pair. For headgear, I use a wool stocking cap that pulls down to cover the face. This is handier than carrying a separate face mask.

Since my hands have been frostbitten, I go for the warmest hand covering I can find. These are heavy wool mittens covered by separate, thick leather mitts. The leather is silicone treated and is so heavy that there is no problem with wet snow. With these mitts on, you can't do much more than hold a ski pole, but they'll keep your hands warm under the most severe conditions.

A pair of waterproof, nylon gaiters go over pants bottoms and boot tops. They will keep the snow out of your boots and also keep the tops of them dry. A pair that reach from the top of the foot to mid-calf will weigh almost nothing.

Into the pack goes the bottom half of the quilted underwear. The top, as noted above, is sometimes worn as a jacket. This underwear is an emergency item for extremely cold days and can be worn to bed on extremely cold nights. Also in the pack is wet gear which consists of light nylon rain chaps and a waterproof, not water repellent, nylon jacket. The jacket should be long enough to cover the top of the chaps. You're not likely to encounter rain, of course, but falling snow can be just as wet. This gear also is handy for keeping dry when digging a snow cave. When wearing wet gear, remember to shed some layers of clothing and pace yourself to avoid excessive sweating.

BOOTS

Winter Hiking Boots

As with tents, there is probably no ideal boot for cold-weather camping. From the standpoint of materials used, there are three types generally worn by winter campers: all leather, all rubber, and a combination of the two. A fourth type, consisting of heavy felt liners covered by a canvas shell with thin leather or felt soles, is suitable only for very dry-cold conditions. That is, in areas where temperatures remain so low that there is no possibility of the snow melting. Such conditions seldom prevail for any length of time, except at high altitudes and in the arctic.

All-leather boots seem to be the most popular, yet they are far from ideal. True, leather is an excellent material for footgear. It is pliable enough to conform to the foot and soft enough to be comfortable. More importantly, it can breathe. This reduces condensation inside the boot, helping to keep feet dry. Yet because it breathes, leather is almost impossible to waterproof. No matter how much mink oil you slather on your boots or how well you spray with silicone, it won't keep them dry for more than a day in wet snow. Even in mid-winter, when temperatures are at their lowest, you'll have problems with snow melting on your boots from the warmth of your feet. And your leather footgear will get progressively wetter each day you are out.

Rubber boots are no better. Rubber is stiff and no amount of walking will ever make it conform to your foot. The tops of the boots will chafe your legs and the material itself is a poor insulator. Moreover, your feet will sweat badly, making your socks as wet as though you were wearing leather.

The combination boots, called pacs, have rubber shoe bottoms that cover the foot to just below the ankle. These are stitched to leather uppers. The idea is that the rubber will keep you dry and the leather tops will permit some breathing. Like all compromises, it isn't perfect, but in most cases pacs are best for cold-weather camping, especially in spring and fall. Certainly, in wet conditions, a quality pac will keep your feet warmer than any leather boot. The best pacs to buy are those that come with a heavy felt liner. The liner provides padding and insulation and also absorbs moisture. Buy an extra liner with your pacs, then while you are wearing one, the other pair can be drying out.

These combination boots are less expensive than a good leather pair, but tend to run slightly heavier. Mine are Sorel brand, and in a size ten, medium width, complete with the liner, they weigh nearly five pounds.

There are some campers who, for one reason or another, won't wear pacs. I used to belong to that group myself and went through a series of leather boots before switching. If you insist on wearing leather, you'll find more boots that are unsatisfactory than are suitable for winter wear. Don't buy those heavy, stiff-soled climbing or mountaineering boots. They are overpriced, weigh a ton, and are designed for cliff hanging, not hiking. Stay with top quality, medium-weight hiking boots. They have flexible soles and even with a glove leather lining, shouldn't weigh more than four pounds in a 10-D size. These will do as well as any leather boot in winter, and can be used equally well for summer hiking.

Ski-touring Boots

If you're a ski tourer, you don't have much option in boots. You'll have to settle for good leather ski boots. Don't buy the low-cut light boots that are designed for racing or cross country. For rugged traveling, you'll want one that comes above the ankle like a hiking boot. It gives better control and protection and can be used for hiking in a pinch.

Treating your boots with grease or silicone spray will help you keep dry. I've found that the silicone, when generously applied, seems to do a better job. In addition, you can buy light rubber covers for your ski boots. The covers are thin enough not to interfere with the bindings. Using both silicone and the covers, you can keep your feet reasonably dry.

Boots for -20 Degrees

I'd avoid boots advertised as being good for temperatures to -20 degrees. They are expensive and impractical for anything but extremely dry-cold conditions, when their highly-touted cold protection is, no doubt, effective. Such conditions seldom occur in snow country. These boots have a layer of foam insulation between the outer leather and the inner lining. When the boot gets wet, the foam soaks up water. My feet have never been colder than in a pair of wet -20 degree boots. And, once wet, the foam makes these boots extremely difficult to dry.

Moreover, the manufacturer recommends that you buy the boot large enough to leave some room around your foot. The purpose is to insure good circulation. An excellent idea, but if the boot allows your foot to move too much, you'll have problems. If you slam your foot into a rock while scrambling down steep pitches, your toes will be jammed into the hard toe of the boot, raising a beautiful set of blood blisters under your toenails. They'll be painful enough to spoil your trip. This has happened to me and several of my friends who bought -20 degree boots. Of course, any hard-toed boot will do the same thing if it is improperly fitted.

How to Fit Boots

When selecting a pair of leather hiking boots, try them on with the same number and kind of socks that you will wear on the trail. Put the boots on without lacing them. Then, while the salesman holds the boot firmly to the floor, try to turn your foot. It should pivot slightly, but the ball of the foot shouldn't move from side to side. Now, push your foot as far forward as possible by lightly kicking the boot against something solid. While you stand straight, let the salesman put his index finger in the boot behind your heel. He should just be able to touch the sole of the boot. Next, kick the boot to move your heel all the way back, then do some knee bends. Your foot should move only a little, no more than an eighth of an inch. Now lace up the boots, firmly, but not tightly. Walk around, jump, climb some stairs, flex your knees. After several minutes, the boots should still feel comfortable.

Given a choice between two pair of equal comfort, take the lightest pair. According to the backpacker's rule, every pound on the foot is like five in the pack.

COOKING GEAR

In winter, it's important to keep cook gear light and simple. If your party consists of more than two campers, you can carry a little extra. But even then, it's best to keep pots and pans to a minimum. You'll need a plate, fork, and spoon for each member of the group. Tin forks and spoons are lightest. The plates should be aluminum, which is preferable to plastic because metal plates can double as lids and can be used for other cooking chores. You'll be drinking plenty of hot fluids, so plastic cups are best, but don't pack them with the rest of the cook gear. Stow them in an outside pocket of the pack where they will be handy to use along the trail.

A ten-inch, Teflon coated, aluminum fry pan and two pots (one-and-a-half and two-quart size) will be plenty for two campers. If pack weight is running on the heavy side, I'll leave the fry pan, since it's easy to plan meals that won't require it. It's best to avoid those expensive aluminum cook sets found in most suppliers' catalogs. Instead, search your favorite discount store for the cheapest, thinnest aluminum pans you can find. They will do the job and are much lighter in the pack than the high priced, thick-walled kind. A plastic bag for each pot will keep the soot from rubbing off inside your pack. Remember, though, to let the pan cool before sticking it in its cover.

With the cook gear, I like to include matches, wrapped tightly in plastic, a combination salt and pepper shaker and a small piece of plastic scrubber. If I'm planning on an open fire for some of the cooking, I'll take a light backpacker's grill. That's it, except for a stove and fuel.

STOVES

Small backpacking stoves burn a variety of fuels, including

Author's cook gear for two men consists of Teflon fry pan, two light aluminum pots (one and one-half quarts each), three aluminum plates, two plastic cups, combo salt and pepper shaker, matches, plastic scrubber, two forks and two spoons. On some trips, the backpacker's seven-ounce grill is included. (Photo by Ray Stebbins)

white gas, alcohol, kerosine, butane, and propane. Butane, of course, can be eliminated for winter use since it freezes at 32 degrees F. Kerosine is acceptable, but because of its low volatility, you have to carry an extra priming fuel to start it. Alcohol is a safe fuel, but I've found it to be very inefficient in cold weather. This leaves us with white gas and propane.

On a trip by myself, or with one other camper, I'll carry the Optimus 8-R, which burns white gas. It is light, at one and three-quarter pounds, and compact enough to slip into an outside pocket of the pack. It is an unusually efficient stove for

The Optimus 8-R, on the right, and the Optimus 111-B, on the left, are excellent backpacking stoves. Note the one-quart fuel can in the background. (Photo by Ray Stebbins)

its size — the small, one third-pint fuel tank will allow about an hour of average cooking. That's why it's one of the most popular small stoves.

The only fuel cans that I trust for white gas are a tinned brass type made in Germany. They are available through most backpacking suppliers. They have a flat profile that allows them to slip easily into an outside pocket on the pack. The sides of the cans are flexible, making it easy to check to see if the caps are on tightly. Just squeeze the sides and if any air escapes, the top isn't tight enough. The threads on the caps are very fine and are easily cross-threaded, so handle them with care. If you have difficulty in getting a cap off, you can improvise a vise.

Just cut and trim flat two pieces of wood about eight inches long. Clamp these around the cap, making a V vise by holding two ends tightly together with one hand and with the other grip the open end of the V and squeeze. Then, holding the can with your knees, use the leverage of the sticks to loosen the cap.

For groups of three or more campers, where the weight of the cooking gear can be divided up, I prefer carrying the Primus "Grasshopper," a propane fueled stove. Complete with gas cylinder that will burn for six hours or more, it weighs only two and a half pounds. This makes it lighter than most of the larger white-gas stoves, even without including the extra weight of their fuel cans. Propane fuel is more expensive and the stoves somewhat less efficient, but they are more convenient. Unlike white-gas stoves, they require no priming.

The Primus "Grasshopper" is light enough for packing and doesn't need priming. (Photo courtesy of Primus-Sievert)

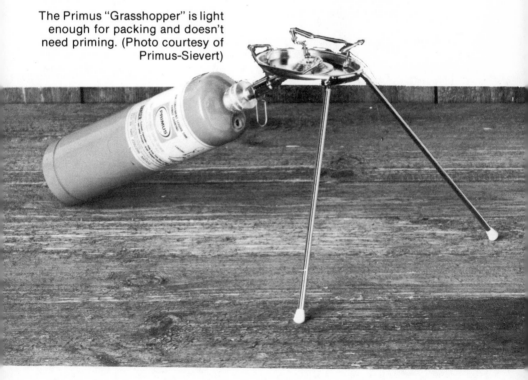

OTHER ESSENTIALS

Fire-building Kit

Even though you don't plan to have open fires, or even if they are not permitted in the area where you plan to camp, carry a fire-building kit. In winter, no experienced outdoorsman ever takes one step away from his vehicle or camp without being absolutely certain he has his fire-making materials *in his pocket.*

As a minimum, a fire kit should contain matches in a waterproof container, some type of starter, and a small amount of tinder. The starter can be a candle, chemical tablets such as hexamine, or a chemical paste. I prefer the paste, since it can be more easily used to prime a white-gas stove. For tinder, you can take a small wad of 000 steel wool, waxed cardboard, or chemically-treated shavings.

Fire-building materials include (left to right) a butane lighter, combination fire starter and tinder sticks, a stearic acid candle, matches in a waterproof container, a pocket fire-starter kit, and matches in a plastic sack. (Photo by Ray Stebbins)

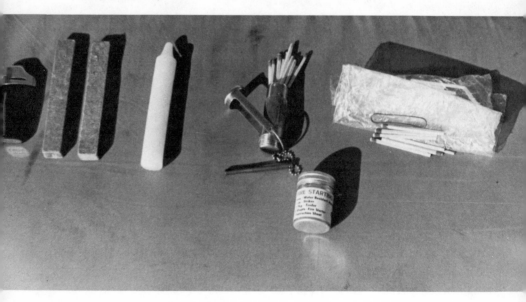

In addition to these items, I carry a non-refillable butane lighter. Kept in an inner shirt pocket, it will stay warm enough to work at low temperatures. I also like to have a Metal Match, which along with your knife, becomes the modern man's flint and steel. It's a life saver if something happens to your matches. For good measure, I carry a stub of plumber's candle that is made with stearic acid, which gives it a hot flame. With these items, you'll have no trouble building a fire, even with wet wood.

Toilet and First-aid Kits

Your toilet kit needn't be elaborate. Mine includes a toothbrush, a small tube of paste, a tube of bio-degradable soap and a Handiwipe for a towel. You will also need some toilet paper to go in the pack and it's a good idea to carry a wad in your pocket as well. You can add any other items you want, but remember you're fighting every ounce of weight.

My first-aid kit is equally sparse. It includes some Band-Aids, two compresses, a small roll of gauze and of adhesive tape, and a plastic bottle of pain pills. I also take a tube of A-fil or similar sun-screen ointment. The screening type ointment is more effective in preventing burn than the tanning type. The sun's rays, reflected from snow, can produce a bad burn right through suntan lotion.

If you will be in an area where water is suspect, you'll want a vial of halazone tablets. A hundred of these small pills will weigh an ounce, and one pill will purify a pint of water in thirty minutes. Halazone tablets have a short shelf-life, and you should be certain that the tablets are less than six months old. They can be purchased at most drugstores.

A good pair of goggles with dark green lenses will be needed to protect your eyes from the snow glare. Dark glasses won't do the job. They let in too much light at the sides and they won't protect against the wind. I like the ski goggles that have interchangeable lenses. This way, I can carry an extra pair of dark ones, in case the first set gets broken, and also a yellow set for those dark days when visibility is poor.

Personal Tools

Carry at least one good knife. Like your matches, it should be with you at all times. I prefer a folding type with two blades, carried in a small case on the belt. The larger of the two blades is four-inches long and heavy enough for any camp chores. I also keep a smaller knife in my pants pocket. Both knives are well sharpened, but I keep a small piece of Arkansas stone in my watch pocket for re-sharpening. Nothing is more frustrating, useless, and possibly dangerous than a dull knife. If you own a sheath knife you might want to try throwing it away. They are awkward to carry, continually banging against the pack frame and always in the way. Nothing marks the greenhorn more surely than one of those six-inch monsters dangling from his belt.

You'll need a good compass. I prefer the lensatic type, but it doesn't have to be that fancy. Just stay away from the cheap ones and make certain that the north needle is clearly marked. There are some around that simply have half of the needle dark and the other half light colored. Though it may seem unlikely — and, of course, it wouldn't happen to you — some campers have been lost when they forgot which color meant north. With the compass, you should have contour maps of the area you will visit. (Map ordering information is in the next chapter.)

There is a small, backpacking flashlight made by Mallory and available from most suppliers. Complete with two batteries, it weighs about three ounces. Batteries won't function at very cold temperatures, so you'll have to carry the light in an inside shirt pocket and take it into your sleeping bag at night to keep it warm.

I include a plastic trowel for digging sanitary pits and an aluminum quart bottle to go in the pack as a canteen. Fifty feet of one-quarter-inch nylon parachute cord weighs about two ounces and is handy for a variety of uses. And, if you are going into avalanche country, dye it bright red so it can be used as avalanche safety cord. At least one member of the group should carry a thermometer, so you can check the still air temperatures to estimate wind chill (see chapter 4).

All of the above items should be in your winter pack each time you go out. There are other items I like to take but they aren't essential. For example, I like to keep records, so I always carry a small notebook and pencil stub. Since I usually plan on open fires, I often include a folding saw that weighs only eight ounces. I never have and never will carry an ax or hatchet. In years of camping in all seasons, I've never had any use for either. There is nothing they can do for me that a saw can't do better and more safely with less weight.

Occasionally, we plan to set up in one area and live in snow caves. On such a trip, I take a break-down aluminum snow-shovel and save some weight by leaving the tent at home. Selection of additional items, if any, will depend on the purpose of your trip. You may want to take a camera and film, fishing gear, predator calls, experimental survival kits, or a little reading matter. A discussion of the various activities that can be enjoyed in a winter camp is reserved for chapter 7.

Author and his friend, Bill Brimmer, unload in preparation for a trip into Wyoming's backcountry. (Photo by Ray Stebbins)

2

How to Get There

Campers who don't live in snow country can reach it fairly easily these days, thanks to the network of public transportation to winter recreation areas that has been developed primarily for skiers. In many areas, especially in Canada, it's possible to load your equipment on a bus, train, or plane and travel directly to your camping site. Of course, using public transportation limits your choice of areas, ties you to a schedule, and increases the cost of camping. So the majority of campers still rely on their own vehicles for transportation.

AUTOMOBILES

Inhabitants of the snow belt are already familiar with the annual chore of winterizing their cars. Each fall, they go through the ritual of switching to a lighter motor oil and lubricants, checking the anti-freeze and, perhaps, changing to snow tires. Often, however, a very important item is overlooked — the battery.

41

Cold temperatures are tough on batteries, and if yours isn't in top condition, it could mean trouble with cold-weather starts. In town, the problem is merely annoying. Winter campers, however, often park in isolated areas, in subzero cold, for days at a time. Under these conditions, a battery with plenty of starting power is essential. Nothing is more disheartening than to return to your car from a winter trek, only to find that your motor won't turn over.

To avoid the problem, make certain that the battery is fully charged and — equally important — that terminals and connections are well cleaned and tightened.

It's also a good idea to check the cold crank rating of your battery against the cubic inch displacement of your engine. This rating is based on the number of amps a new battery will deliver over a period of thirty seconds to start an engine at 0 degrees F. Many cars, especially the smaller models, come with batteries that have the same cold crank rating as the cubic inch displacement of the motor. This is a minimum. And any vehicle that is to be parked outside in below zero temperatures should have a battery rating higher than the engine displacement. The greater the difference, the more reliability and starting power the battery will have. Also, the larger the engine and the more power accessories carried, the greater the difference should be. To determine the proper rating for your vehicle, check with your local garage or battery specialist.

For added insurance, cold-weather campers should carry, in the trunk of their car, the usual gear hauled by all experienced winter drivers. This would include a shovel, a large bucket of sand (its weight aids traction in normal driving; thrown under tires it prevents wheel-spinning on ice), tire chains, jumper cables, a tow chain, and road flares or reflectors.

Learning the proper speed for various road conditions and how to drive in problem situations come only with actual experience. And experience plus careful maintenance, along with caution and common sense, can make winter driving about as safe and trouble free as summer travel usually is.

In addition to transportation to his selected area, the cold-weather camper will generally need some means of traveling over the snow. A single experience with hiking through deep drifts will convince anyone that snowshoes, skis, or snow machines are an absolute necessity for getting around in snow country.

SNOWSHOES

Though often considered dull and unglamorous when compared to skis, snowshoes should be the most popular method of over-the-snow travel. They are, by far, the most economical gear. They are easy to use and require no formal instruction. An hour or so of practice usually will enable anyone to handle them with reasonable skill.

Types of Snowshoes

There are three basic types of snowshoe design: the Alaskan trail, the Maine or Michigan trail, and the bearpaw. The Alaskan style, sometimes called the pickerel because of their long, thin shape, are generally about ten inches wide and fifty-six inches long. They were developed for use in open country, powder snow, and on well-defined trails. This type features an upturned toe and a long tail for trailing. This means that the tail acts as a rudder as it drags in the snow, keeping the shoe lined up with the trail. It also serves as a counter weight. The snowshoer needs only to lift his foot slightly and the weight of the tail brings the toe up, clear of the snow. This results in a considerable saving of energy.

The Maine or Michigan model is wider and not so long. Sizes vary, but an average is about fifteen inches wide and forty-two to forty-eight inches long. These shoes also offer a turned-up toe and a tail for trailing. They were designed to use in forested areas with little underbrush.

The bearpaw, as its name implies, is a tailless, ovate shoe

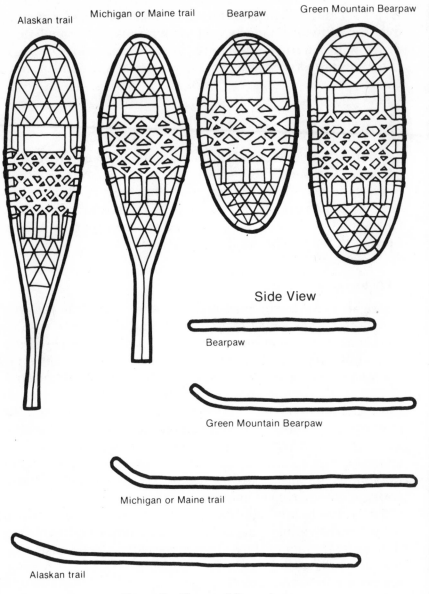

Figure 3.   Types of Snowshoes

that is usually flat, though one model does have a slightly turned-up toe. Made for use in brushy areas, the bearpaw is somewhat more maneuverable than trail snowshoes. Because of its compact size, this type of snowshoe is often carried by snowmobilers for emergency use. Yet, due to its small surface area and poor performance on trails, the bearpaw is not a good choice for the winter backpacker. This shoe is particularly bad in powder snow, and its wide form forces you to walk like a saddle-sprung cowboy. Even if you are operating out of a base camp with only a day pack, you'd be better off with one of the longer styles.

The Michigan or Maine shoe also is wide enough to be uncomfortable for the beginner. In other respects, however, it is a good trail shoe. The shorter length makes this style slightly more maneuverable than the Alaskans. On the other hand, except in the largest sizes, it won't support as much weight as the longer shoe. But it's certainly preferable to the bearpaw and is popular with many snowshoers.

For the backpacker, however, the Alaskan style offers some definite advantages. First and foremost, it will support more weight than any other type of snowshoe. Though I am of average size, my winter pack and heavy clothing will often bring my total weight to 220 pounds. It takes a large snowshoe to support this weight, especially in powder snow. Moreover, with practice, the longer, thinner shoes are easier to use. Once the camper has developed that long, rolling, snowshoe stride, he won't need to walk spraddle-legged. Finally, the Alaskan is especially good for fast traveling on well developed trails.

Most of the objections to the Alaskan style center on its weight and lack of maneuverability. Yet the weight difference isn't that great when compared to any snowshoe large enough to support a camper and his pack. As for maneuverability, I find the Alaskan easier to thread through thick stands of trees than the wider shoes, and I've taken a pair through dense forests of lodgepole pine with little difficulty. From my own experience, I'd be inclined to recommend the Alaskan trail style as the first choice for the serious backpacker.

Construction and Maintenance

Most snowshoes available today are still made with wooden frames and rawhide webbing. Some manufacturers are offering shoes made with aluminum framing and neoprene rubber webbing. They are more expensive and, unless they were at least two pounds lighter than my five-pound Alaskans, I wouldn't be willing to pay the extra cost. Plastic snowshoes, so far, haven't proved reliable for trail use. I'd avoid them regardless of any advantage in price or weight. All of which means that the traditional wood and rawhide shoe is still a good choice. Given proper care, such shoes will provide years of service.

Snowshoe bindings have traditionally been made of leather and some campers still use them. Leather, however, has some drawbacks, the most serious being the fact that it absorbs snow melt and stretches when wet. This results in loose bindings, which are both bothersome and dangerous. When you take off your snowshoes, the wet leather bindings quickly freeze, making them difficult to put on again. I switched long ago to a neoprene-nylon combination. The nylon, between two layers of neoprene, prevents stretching and the neoprene won't freeze.

There are various types of bindings. I prefer the kind that have a toe web that keeps the boot from moving forward. For better lateral control, pick a binding that has a double toe strap and an instep strap that buckles. In any case, I'd avoid leather or plastic bindings.

Proper maintenance of wood and rawhide snowshoes is simple and consists mainly of keeping a good coat of top grade varnish on both frame and webs. When in use, snowshoes should always be left out in the cold so that any snow or ice left on them won't melt and soak the webbing. When being stored after use, they should be cleaned, thoroughly dried and then varnished.

Despite their awkward appearance, you may be surprised to find that snowshoes make carrying a pack easier than hiking with a pack. Most experienced snowshoers use ski

The best snowshoe bindings are made of a neoprene-nylon sandwich. The bindings pictured are handmade by Beck Outdoor Projects and offer excellent design and quality materials. (Photo by Ray Stebbins)

poles. Though many start without them, if they do much backpacking, they soon acquire a set. Poles are not only an aid in rough terrain and a necessity for navigating steep pitches, they also are useful in probing suspected snow bridges or weak ice.

SKI TOURING

Ease of travel added to the comparatively low price and quick, easy development of technique, should make snowshoes the most popular form of over-the-snow travel. Such is not the case. The rapid development of ski touring, along with the elitist mystique imparted by the mere possession of a pair of slats, has kept ski sales well ahead of the pedestrian webs.

However, ski touring has more going for it than mere mystique. It is, first of all, fun. Few activities are more enjoyable than gliding effortlessly on skis through powder snow in the cotton-candy world of winter.

Though the equipment required costs several times more than snowshoes, it is much less expensive than that needed for downhill skiing. You can completely outfit yourself for touring for about half the price of a good set of downhill skis alone. Moreover, anyone who is reasonably well coordinated can master most of the basic techniques required for touring with only a few hours of instruction. Formal lessons are not an absolute necessity. If you have a friend who is an experienced tourer, he can probably give you enough instruction to get you started.

For the winter camper, however, ski touring also has some disadvantages. While it is relatively easy to tour without a pack, or with only a small day pack, it is another matter to ski with a fullsized packsack. A thirty-five or forty pound load on your back tends to destroy balance and control. It takes a fairly polished skier to handle it with ease. For the beginner, a backpack complicates the process of learning touring techniques. He must first master the basics, then learn them all over again with the pack on his back.

Touring increases the risk of such injuries as twists, sprains, and fractures, especially for the beginner. Such accidents can incapacitate the summer camper, but in the winter wilderness, they can have serious consequences. The safe approach is to develop skill before you travel in the back country and guard against trying to ski beyond your abilities.

Although some skiers enjoy it, I have to think of waxing as a disadvantage. For me, the chores of applying and scraping wax have always been a pain in the nether parts. But there are some ways of easing this dull task; we'll discuss them in the next section.

This commentary is not intended to discourage ski touring. On the contrary, I'd advise every cold-weather camper to rent touring gear and try it, at least twice. Ski-touring equipment can be rented at most winter recreation areas and in many sporting goods stores. Purveyors have found that rentals often lead to sales since it's easy to get hooked on touring.

Skis

Modern touring skis are a compromise between heavy mountaineering types and the light, cross country or racing style. To give you an idea of the range in skis, the light racing and cross country style will vary from 40 mm to 52 mm wide, while the heavy mountaineering types will range from 65 to 75 mm in width. The camper who intends to carry a pack will need sturdy skis that are long and broad enough to give him good support on the snow. Suitable backpacking skis will average 55 to 60 mm in width.

Touring skis are rather long. The tip of the ski should reach the wrist or knuckle of your upstretched arm and hand. I'm five foot eleven and the right length for me would be about 205 cm.

To insure longer wear and, more importantly, better control under various conditions of snow and terrain, your skis should have hard edges. Most touring skis use aluminum, full-length or in segments, or full-length lignostone. The latter is made of beechwood which has been soaked with phenolic resin and compressed under great pressure, producing a light, very hard material. I prefer the lignostone edges, but either type will do. Usually, the rest of the running surface of a good touring ski is made of hickory.

There also are skis available that require no waxing. One uses dual mohair strips on the bottom and the other has a plastic base with an imprinted fishscale pattern that glides forward but holds against the back thrust. Though I dislike the job of waxing, I can't recommend any waxless ski. The plastic types won't work as well as a waxed bottom and the plastic

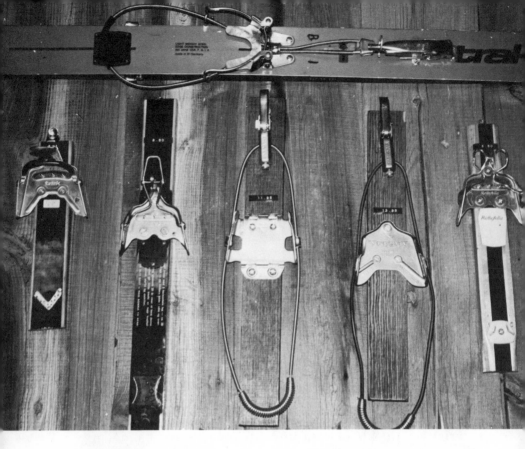

Shown here are three pin-type bindings and three cable-type bindings. Pin-type bindings with heel plates hold only the toe of the boot; they are popular for touring. However, the author prefers cable bindings since they give better control. (Photo courtesy of Milt McLaskey and Dana Van Burgh)

tends to wear and lose its holding ability. The mohair types work reasonably well in warmer weather, 25 degrees F. and higher, but will not perform as well as waxed skis in colder temperatures.

Accessories

The ski tourer uses a cable type binding. There are various styles, but they have in common a toe plate and a locking device that clamps the toe of the boot to the ski and a cable that fits around the back of the boot, usually into a groove in the heel. For better control, the binding should also have a heel plate to prevent the boot from sliding sideways off the ski on

Here are three types of ski poles (left to right) bamboo, fiberglass, and aluminum. (Photo courtesy of Milt McLaskey and Dana Van Burgh)

turns. I like the "popper" type with a rubber center that springs up when you raise your heel. This helps keep the snow from building up under your boot. The idea of a cable binding is to allow raising the heel from the ski to stride, yet provide control on turns. Some types are made to be used with regular hiking boots. However, I'd recommend the purchase of regular ski boots (see Chapter 1, Part II). This gives you a greater choice of bindings and, I feel, a more secure fastening.

Ski poles, of course, are essential for touring. They should be long enough to just fit under your outstretched arm. If they are slightly shorter, it won't matter. Bamboo, aluminum, and fiberglass have all been used in making poles. The bamboo are generally less expensive, with aluminum in the middle and fiberglass the most expensive. Some tourers feel that both the bamboo and fiberglass, being more springy, give more thrust on the forward stride. It's probably true, but I have more confidence in the strength of metal, so that's what I use. For the average skier, I doubt that it makes much difference.

Waxing

Though I admit I don't enjoy it, waxing is a very necessary part of ski touring and can make the difference between a good day on the trail and a miserable one. A properly waxed ski that performs on the trail is a pleasure well worth the effort. But some skiers get carried away by their involvement with waxing technique. They end up toting pounds of waxes, heaters, scrapers, thermometers, wind gauges and charts. Generally, they spend more time waxing than skiing. At the other extreme are those who slap on any wax that's handy and eventually cover it with a soft wax. They conclude that skis are useless unless you're going downhill.

The answer lies somewhere between the two extremes. Ideally, the properly waxed ski will glide forward smoothly but stick firmly to the snow on the back thrust, even when climbing a sharp slope. The problem is that snow varies greatly in its age, structure, and moisture content. A number of different waxes are required for various snow conditions and temperatures.

Basically, waxes are divided into two groups, hard and soft. The former are called simply "hard waxes" and the soft are called klisters. Each type comes in a variety of grades that are color coded as to recommended use. Generally, the newer the snow and the lower the temperature, the harder the wax needed. Conversely, the older the snow and the warmer the temperature, the softer the wax should be. Klisters are used for wet or crusty snow. It is best to stay with the same brand of wax so that you get to know its characteristics as indicated by its color code. A beginner probably is better off staying with

Swix or Rex waxes since they are widely distributed and available almost everywhere.

If you have new skis, the bottoms will have to be prepared by application of a base wax. The idea is to completely seal the wood against moisture. There are some brands that are merely sprayed or painted on the ski. Better and longer lasting are the tar base preparations called "warm-in" bases. These require the application of heat. Before applying any base, the bottoms of your skis should be cleaned to the wood. With new skis, this often means sanding off the protective coat of varnish with fine sandpaper.

When the bottoms are smoothed and clean, place the skis in a steady position where you can work over them from tip to tail. Starting at the tip, apply the base by spraying or painting it on with a brush. Cover the bottoms completely. If you are using a warm-in base, take a small torch and heat the applied base until it bubbles. Keep the torch constantly moving so it won't scorch the wood. After you have heated the first coat, apply another. This time, as you heat the second coat, boil only a few inches at a time. When a section is bubbling, remove the torch and quickly wipe off the excess base with a rag. When you have attained a smooth, glassy finish, place the skis outside to cool and dry before putting on any running wax.

When in doubt about which running wax to apply, always start with a harder one. If you're wrong, you can rub a softer wax over the harder one, but the reverse is impossible. Rub the wax over the entire bottom of the ski with an up and down motion (don't put wax in the groove of the ski). Apply only a thin coat and rub it down to a glossy finish with a waxing cork. Remember, easy does it. Several thin layers are more effective than one thick coat.

It will take five to ten minutes of skiing for your wax to set. Only then can you tell if you've chosen the right one. If you skip when climbing, the wax is too hard and if you can't glide smoothly, the wax is too soft. Before changing waxes, however, try applying another coat of the same wax and see if that helps. If your wax is still too hard, try applying a softer wax on

Waxing kit used by Bill Brimmer, a skiing expert, consists of four hard waxes and a rubbing cork. (Photo by Ray Stebbins)

the bottom area just under your foot and on the back end of the ski. If it still slips, then rub the softer wax over the entire ski. If your wax is too soft, you'll have to take it off before you can apply a harder one.

Most hard waxes can be applied out in the cold, but klisters must be applied at room temperatures or heated if used outdoors. Wax manufacturers supply detailed instructions for the use of their products, which is a great aid in selecting the right wax.

Experience and familiarity with their skiing areas enable most ski tourers to limit the number of waxes they carry to a half dozen or less. In fact, Bill Brimmer, a camping partner of mine, who is a certified instructor and formerly trained troops in Alaska in the tactical use of skis, takes only three waxes, all hard. These usually include a red for damp snow, a blue for colder snow, and a green for very dry, cold conditions. He never uses a klister.

However, Bill does carry mohair climbing skins. In the mountains where steep climbs are the rule, mohair or imitation seal skins are used by most skiers. These "skins" are

Bill Brimmer attaches mohair "skins" in preparation for some steep climbing. (Photo by Ray Stebbins)

attached to the bottom of the skis. The nap remains flat and smooth on the forward glide, but the back thrust is against the grain, forcing the nap to stand up and dig into the snow. This enables the skier to climb steep grades without slipping.

For anyone who becomes involved in touring, I'd recommend *The Regnery Guide to Ski Touring* by Sven Wiik and David Sumner. Wiik is a former Olympic Nordic Skiing coach and the dean of touring in the Rockies. David Sumner, an old friend, is a knowledgeable outdoorsman and a writer of consummate skill. Their book was responsible for my renewed interest in touring.

Campers in the eastern states may also want to obtain a copy of the *Ski Touring Guide,* a booklet put out by the Eastern Ski Association, 22 High Street, Brattleboro, Vermont 05301. It offers a thorough listing of tour areas in the East as well as other useful information. It is presently available from the association for $2.00.

Skis vs. Snowshoes

Leaving aside previous considerations of cost and complications, which is best in terms of pure mobility — skis or snowshoes? The answer, of course, will depend to some extent on the temperament of the camper, but more perhaps on the kind of terrain he will travel. In most circumstances, skis are faster and require less effort. In open, rolling country, skis are ideal and, with climbing skins, will even handle mountain terrain. Snowshoes, on the other hand, are safer, more stable and have a definite advantage on long, steep climbs, especially when you are carrying a heavy pack. They also are easier to use in brush and heavy timber.

By using both, you can cover any type of terrain in any circumstance. If you feel you have to make a choice, however, I'd suggest renting both types of equipment and trying them to determine which is the best for you.

There is, of course, a third alternative for over-the-snow travel — the snowmobile.

SNOWMOBILES

My first experience with snow machines was the result of a magazine assignment to do an article on Montana's Big Sky Trail. Located in the southwestern part of the state, this 120-mile snowmobile trail runs between Bozeman and West Yellowstone. It is reputed to have sections as rugged as any in the West. Though I had never ridden a machine, the hearty and experienced members of the Gallatin Valley Snowmobile Club managed to get me through. At the end of two days, even my toenails were tired.

Like many others who had never ridden before, I had assumed that the major advantage of the snowmobile was that it required no effort on the part of the operator. This might be the case if all snow country were flat and all of its snow firm and fully packed. It isn't, and riding a snowmobile in really

Snowmobilers on Montana's Big Sky Trail break for lunch. (Photo by Ray Stebbins)

The snowmobile camper is concerned with bulk not weight. With a sled, he can pack in a deluxe camp. (Photo courtesy of Government of Quebec, Department of Tourism)

rugged terrain can be even more demanding than skiing or snowshoeing in the same area. With experience, snowmobiling gets easy, but there still are times when it is a very rough sport.

The snowmobile offers certain unique advantages for the winter camper. Foremost is the fact that you won't have to carry your pack. It can be tied down in the passenger space of the snowmobile seat. This means that the snowmobiler needn't be overly concerned with weight, only bulk. Therefore, he can take more gear and a greater variety of food and other comforts into the back country with little effort. If he is traveling in gentle terrain, he can haul a cargo sled behind the machine. In it, he can carry a deluxe camping outfit, complete with large umbrella tent, stoves, heaters, and all of the groceries he could possibly want.

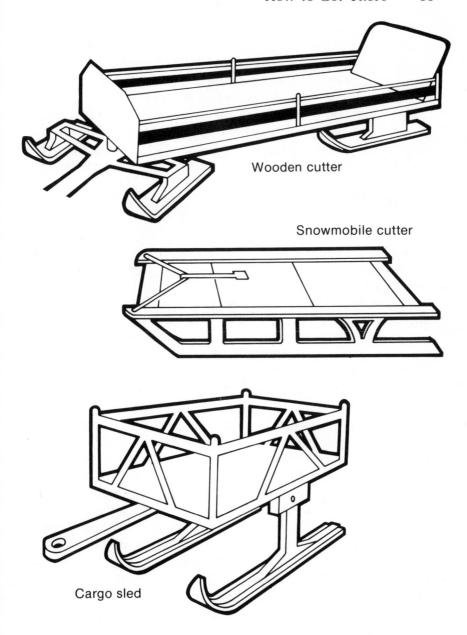

Wooden cutter

Snowmobile cutter

Cargo sled

Figure 4. Snowmobile sleds

The snowmobile is particularly handy for the ice fisherman, hunter, or serious photographer who must carry additional heavy equipment. Moreover, it will get him into the back country more quickly, leaving him more time to do his outdoor thing. Finally, snowmobiling is fun in itself.

However, there are some disadvantages too. The most obvious of these is the expense. A snowmobile represents a large investment, and you need a small trailer to haul the machine to the jump-off point. Fees, licensing, insurance, and maintainance all add to the cost of snowmobiling. The sport is the most strictly regulated of all winter activities. As a snowmobiling camper, you will be limited to certain areas and your travels will be carefully controlled by various restrictions on the use of your machine. It is definitely not a sport for the loner. Snowmobiling lends itself more to group participation than to solo jaunts.

To discover if snow machines are for you, the best bet is to rent one and try it. Many winter resorts now specialize in snowmobile trips. They provide rental machines, clothing, guides, and instructions for beginners.

If you find that you enjoy riding a machine, try renting one for a camping trip. You may decide that renting is the most economical route to go.

In the event you decide to buy one, do two things before making your purchase. First, ride a variety of rental machines in all kinds of terrain. This will help you determine the size and type best suited to you. Sure, this experiment can be expensive, but it will save you from making a more costly mistake. Next, contact the nearest snowmobile club and spend some time talking to the members. You'll find that snowmobilers are friendly folks and are more than willing to talk about their sport. Hear what they have to say, not only about the machines but about dealers, warranties, parts and service. Only when you have some definite ideas as to which dealers to contact, should you actually go shopping. With seventy manufacturers offering a variety of machines (one has twenty-nine different models) with a host of accessories and options,

Ski-Doo Snowmobile lineup from Bombardier Limited. It gives you an idea of the variety potential snowmobile owners have to choose from. (Photo courtesy of Bombardier Limited)

preselecting a few dealers, who are well recommended, will narrow down the field.

Take your time. Get as much riding experience as you can before you buy. Do plenty of shopping and comparing. The right machine can make the difference between enjoyment of the sport and the belated decision that the sport isn't for you.

Only a year ago, it would have been easy to recommend a snowmobile for the average camper. He would want a model of "standard" size, something between the 200-pound compact and the 500-pound deluxe job. This would have been a machine of about 300 pounds — still light enough to man-handle — with a 350 cc, air-cooled engine turning up around 20 horsepower, and with a track seventeen or eighteen inches wide. Such advice is already outdated.

Today, tracks are going back to fifteen inches, weights are dropping and the muscle of the new 350 cc, liquid-cooled engines is more like 40 horsepower. In fact, the liquid-cooled engine is coming in faster than the rotary engine, which had been expected to dominate the field.

Advocates of the new liquid-cooled engines claim that they deliver smoother power, last longer, are more reliable, and run

Members of a Wilderness Society group set out together on an organized winter trek. (Photo courtesy of the Wilderness Society)

far more quietly. My own experience with air-cooled motors would sell me on the liquid-cooled jobs without any argument. I'd still hold out for 300 pounds or less, so long as the machine was large enough to provide room for my pack. The 350 cc, 40 horsepower would be more than adequate, even when pulling a cargo sled.

The real problem arises when it comes to a choice of options. Some of the newer machines offer improved suspension, higher windshields, headlights mounted on the steering column, eye level instrumentation, better seats, and less noise. Fuel tanks, which often caused weight balance problems, since they were side-mounted, have been centered on some machines. Motors have stronger and lower mountings. All of these features result in easier and safer riding.

Snowmobiling isn't for everyone, any more than is skiing or snowshoeing. There are those who feel that the snow machine has no place in the back country. Others simply don't like machines. Mostly it's a matter of temperament. Rather than take someone else's opinion, try it yourself and decide.

Certainly, for anyone who is unable or unwilling to carry a pack, the snowmobile can be the best route to the full enjoyment of winter camping.

If, however, you have never gone into the snow country by any method, I would suggest that you try them all. Once you have found the mode of travel that suits you best, you will realize that getting there is a good part of the fun.

Bill Brimmer and author check out topographic maps before setting out. Each member of the group should have his own map quadrangle. (Photo by Ray Stebbins)

3

How to Get Started

With all of the necessary equipment gathered, you're ready to set up your first trip. The selection of foods, choosing a suitable area and, if backpacking, picking a good route, are important. If you already have experience with summer camping, you know that a successful trip requires planning and preparation. This is even more true of winter camping. In addition, the cold-weather camper will need to know some compass basics and something about winter weather. However, before he even begins to plan he should assess his physical condition.

CONDITIONING

Ideally, the winter camper should be in excellent physical shape. The average citizen, however, especially those of us over forty, tend to take on the form and toughness of an overstuffed sofa. For those of strong and determined character, the solution is simple: Cut the calories, and from your local high school or college coach, local ski instructor, YMCA or library, get a set of limbering strengthening exercises. Use them faithfully for at least a month before you go.

Unfortunately, for those who, like the author, have will power as strong as a wet paper sack, there is no easy way. Bored by exercising, we have to do our toughening on the trail. This means putting up with some fatigue and sore muscles for the first few winter trips.

Actually, if you stay fairly active during the year hunting, fishing, playing tennis, or participating in other active sports, you shouldn't have much of a problem. Anyone over forty who hasn't had a recent checkup, would be well advised to see his doctor. Tell him what you plan to do. Explain that you'll be carrying a pack, traveling on skis or snowshoes, probably over rough terrain. He will undoubtedly tell you that such activities can be very demanding on the heart and muscles unaccustomed to strenuous exercise. He'll advise you to take it easy and not to overdo it. As long as you follow his advice, there is no reason you can't enjoy winter camping at any age. After all, it doesn't require any particular toughness or stamina, just reasonably good health. I know of one ski tourer, nearly seventy, who can easily outdistance me on the trail.

PLANNING

Once you're satisfied that health is no problem, you're ready to select an area and perhaps an alternate or two. If you plan to use a base camp or a recreational vehicle (RV), there should be plenty of information available from your local state or provincial tourist office. Of course, friends or acquaintances who are cold-weather campers also can provide suggestions. With some areas in mind, you'll want to check to make certain that roads will be plowed and open and that there will be parking places cleared. RVers will want to know what facilities, if any, are available and make reservations for space, if necessary. Food won't be much of a problem since you're not fighting weight and you can take whatever you like.

More detailed information on base camps is included in Chapter 6.

Campers who want to live in the snow but are new to winter camping might be interested in a guided trip. Some organized winter trips are offered by such groups as the Wilderness Society, the National Hiking and Ski Touring Association, and a growing number of private outfitters. More winter resorts are providing group trips for skiers, snowshoers, and snowmobilers, too. Generally, ten to fifteen campers are taken out together under the leadership of an experienced and qualified guide who has charge of all planning and arrangements for food and equipment. All you have to do is bring your personal gear. There usually is a flat fee that includes everything except transportation to the meeting place. On most trips, in addition to furnishing such equipment as skis, snowshoes, or snow machines, the sponsoring organization furnishes instructions on the equipment's use. Trips are rated according to the abilities and physical conditioning required. They range in difficulty from simple trips for the beginner to advanced mountaineering treks.

If you are a little doubtful about your first outing, this might be a good way to get started. The only drawbacks are cost and the limited number of trips available. Moreover, you won't have quite the satisfaction that is derived from a trip you plan yourself.

If you're of a more independent mind (most winter campers are) and want to handle it yourself, then try and take your first trip with a friend who has some experience. If that isn't possible, get at least one other camper to go with you, even if he has no experience. At this point, most books on camping advise you not to go alone, ever. I've never agreed. Certainly, it's more fun to go with someone, but even if I couldn't find a partner, I'd rather go alone than not at all. In such cases, however, I'd advise either hiking or using snowshoes. Avoid skis unless you're an accomplished skier. Also, you will want to avoid any difficult or dangerous terrain and use plenty of caution and good common sense.

Snowmobilers going into the wilderness should always travel in groups. On a snow machine you can get so far into the back country in one day that, in the event of a breakdown, it might be very difficult to get out on your own.

That first trip should be a short one, perhaps a weekend, and preferably in an area you already know from summer camping.

MAPS

An important part of the planning for all winter camping trips is the acquisition and study of contour or topographic maps of the area in which you will be traveling. These maps should be ordered as soon as you have decided where to go.

Obtaining Maps

Canadian contour or topographic maps are available from the Map Distribution Office, Department of Energy, Mines, and Resources, Ottawa, Canada. For U.S. contour maps covering the states east of the Mississippi River, write the Distribution Section, U.S. Geological Survey, 1200 South Eads Street, Arlington, Virginia 22202. For states west of the Mississippi, write the Distribution Section, U.S. Geological Survey, Federal Center, Building 41, Denver, Colorado 80225. Ask for the index map of the areas in which you are interested. The index is a large overlay map indicating the topo sheets available for a given area. It will be sent, along with ordering information and current prices.

The most popular topo maps are those in the seven-and-a-half-minute series, a designation that determines the map scale. In these series, about two and five-eighths inches on the map represents one mile on the ground. The contour interval is a mere twenty feet. These highly detailed maps are the easiest to use and should be ordered when available. Unfortunately, not all areas of the United States are covered by this scale. The next best is the fifteen-minute series. On these maps, approximately one inch equals a mile on the ground. The contour interval is eighty feet. Smaller scale maps are often provided for areas that have not been remapped for some time. While more difficult to use, they are still preferable to any non-contoured map.

The contour lines help you visualize the country. Shown in brown on the USGS maps, each line indicates all of the points of the same elevation in the area. If you walked a circle around the top of a hill, staying always at the same height, your path would form a contour line. When the lines are very close together on the map, a sharp, steep slope is indicated. When widely separated, they signify fairly level country. With practice, you can soon learn to visualize the shape of the land from one of these maps.

In addition to showing lakes, streams, peaks, swamps, and other geographic features, these maps also indicate buildings, trails, abandoned mines, and other manmade objects. All but the oldest maps are colored, with water in blue, woods in green, and open areas in white. All of this, of course, is invaluable in selecting routes.

If you are traveling cross country a good contour map is essential, and each member of the party should have one. If you plan to camp in a state or provincial park or forest, trail maps usually are available. You can either contact the park or forest headquarters or your local tourist bureau to obtain them. Generally they will be sent free of charge. While these maps can be helpful in planning your route, they do not show contour. Contour maps are inexpensive and a wise investment.

Map Orientation

When you receive your contour or topo maps, you'll find, on the border, a V-shaped diagram. One leg will be marked with a star, or the words *True North;* the other will be marked MG (magnetic north). The angle between them is the angle of declination, or the number of degrees that magnetic north

This map is oriented to magnetic north. The dark line on the map is an extension of the magnetic north symbol to make the job of orienting easier. (Photo by Ray Stebbins)

varies from true north in the area covered by the map. For practical purposes, most outdoorsmen use magnetic north to orient their maps, since that's where the compass needle points. To make it easier, I like to take a pencil and straightedge and extend the north magnetic line of the V symbol onto the map, ten inches or so.

When you arrive at your starting point in the field, find a level spot to lay out your map. Make certain you don't have any metal on you that might affect the compass reading. You can check this by backing away several feet. Then as you approach the compass, watch the needle. If it moves, check your pockets and get rid of any sizeable metal objects before you take readings.

Set the compass on top of the map and let the needle settle to point north. Now turn the compass base until the north marking of the compass lines up with the needle. Then, holding the compass firmly, rotate the map until the extended north magnetic line and the compass needle are parallel. The map is now oriented and all land features and directions on the ground correspond with those on the map. Take your time and try to establish in your mind the general lay of the land in relation to where you are on the map. Check out the location of any geographical features such as peaks, streams, trails and old logging roads, noting their general direction.

Route Planning

For your first trip or so, whether you're using a base camp or traveling, it's a good idea to stay with clearly marked trails and to avoid any cross country jaunts. This doesn't mean that you should only use your compass to orient your map. Even when you stay on marked trails, your map and compass can be very handy. The first few trips will give you a chance to develop skill in using them.

In planning your route, your base camp or starting point should be located on a base line. This can be any manmade or natural land feature that runs for some distance in a more or less straight line. It could be a river, stream, ridge, trail, highway, logging road, or any other feature clearly indicated on the map. If you should get lost, it will help you find your way back more quickly.

Here's how: Suppose you have located your parking spot or base camp on Clear Creek, which flows through the area roughly north to south. You plan to go into Lake Whatsit. In planning your route, you draw a straight line from the center of

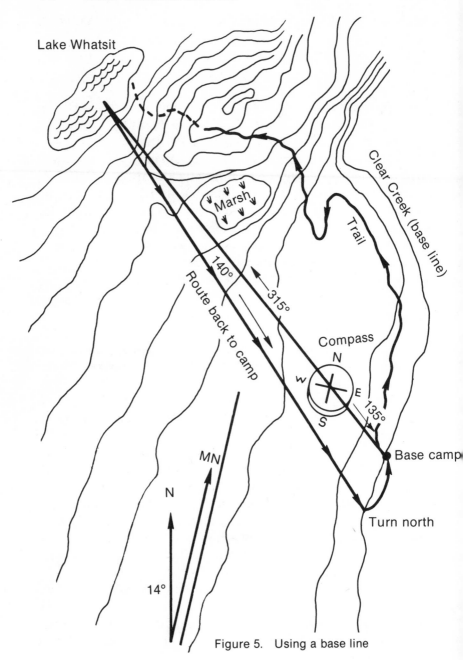

Figure 5.   Using a base line

the lake to your base camp on Clear Creek. Then with the map oriented to magnetic north, place the center of the compass on the line you've drawn to the lake. Making certain the map doesn't move from its oriented position, rotate the compass until the north-pointing needle lines up with the north marking on the edge of the compass. The magnetic north line drawn on the map and the compass needle should be parallel. Now read the number of degrees where the line you've drawn from camp to lake intersects the edge of the compass on the side toward the lake. Let's say it reads 315 degrees or due NW. This is the compass bearing you would follow if you were cutting across country. From the lake back to your camp, you would bear SE or 135 degrees. Write these degree bearings on your route line from the lake to the camp.

Suppose that when you actually reach your base camp or parking area in the field, you don't use the compass bearing. Instead, you follow a trail into Lake Whatsit. It turns out to be a faint trail and poorly marked, but you manage to make it into the lake. On the way back, however, you somehow miss the trail or lose it. After retracing your steps and casting about for a while, you still can't find it. The only way out is to travel cross country by compass.

From the previous calculations marked on your map, you see that the compass bearing from the lake to your base camp was 135 degrees. However, since you are not certain now whether you are north or south of the original line and since there will be some variations in your sightings, you don't want to go back exactly on your original bearing. The chances are you wouldn't hit your base camp by following 135 degrees. You would, of course, hit Clear Creek, but there would be no way of knowing whether to turn north or south to find your camp. You could walk up the creek for twenty minutes and if you didn't find the camp, walk downstream for forty minutes, but this could involve a lot of extra hiking.

You can solve this problem by following a bearing a few degrees to the east or south of the 135-degree line. Looking at the map, you see that by heading a few degrees east, you might

cut the trail. However, there is a large swamp and other obstacles along that route that would have to be avoided. But the country you cross if you head a few degrees south of 135 looks fairly open and easy to travel. Again, you won't hit your base camp, but as this route will bring you out south of the camp, when you hit Clear Creek, you know you'll head north to find your base.

To travel along any bearing line, steady your compass needle on north and sight across the face of the compass along the bearing line you want to follow. Sight on a nearby land feature and walk directly to it. Then take another sighting and so on, until you reach your objective. It's easier if your compass has some type of aiming device. If it doesn't, a pencil or straight stick laid across the compass face, along the bearing line will help you sight.

If you encounter an obstacle, such as a lake or marsh, take your bearing across it to some easily identified object on the other side. Then pick the best route around the obstacle to reach that object and take your next sighting from there. If you are blocked by a high cliff or similar impediment, you'll have to use your compass to get around it. If you're heading north, for example, and you see from the map that you can get around the cliff by heading 30 degrees east of north, then take your bearing at 30 degrees and follow it. Travel at a steady pace and time yourself carefully. When you've cleared it, head back 30 degrees west of north. Travel at the same pace for the same amount of time, then go back to your original north bearing.

Even when using trails, you should keep your compass handy and develop the habit of using it to check landmarks and your location as you travel. It's also a good idea to time your rate of travel over various types of terrain. Later, when you are going cross country by compass, you'll be using time as well as distance to locate your position.

In addition to drawing the bearing lines on your contour

(Facing page) Bill Brimmer sights his lensatic compass on a bearing line to our first objective. (Photo by Ray Stebbins)

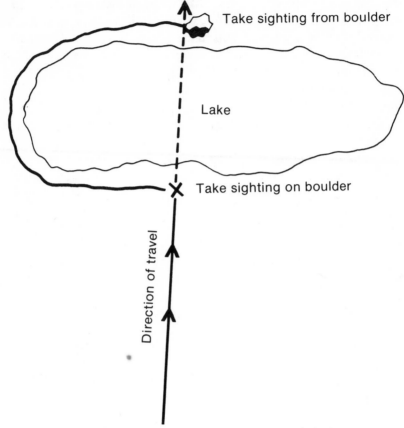

Figure 6.   Sighting a compass over an obstacle

map before leaving home, you also should sketch a time and route map to leave behind with someone who knows your plans. Then, if you don't return as scheduled, an accurate search can be started promptly. This sketch should include the route you'll take, along with any important landmarks, and it should show the dates and locations of each place you plan to use as a campsite.

When planning your routes and side trips, be realistic. Don't overestimate how far you can travel. Winter days are short and it's far better to reach your objective early than late.

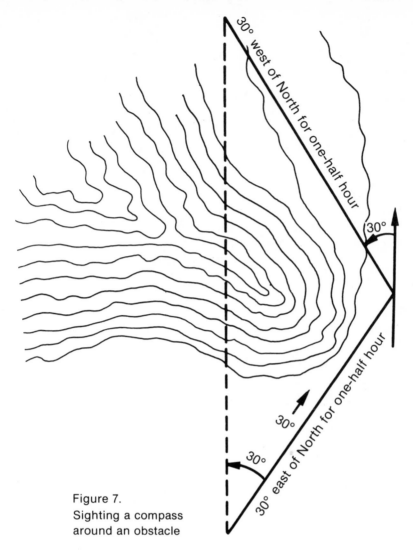

Figure 7.
Sighting a compass
around an obstacle

Remember it takes time and energy to set up a winter camp. For the beginner, only a few miles a day on skis or snowshoes can be more than enough. Even the toughened and experienced winter camper seldom tries for more than four or five miles per day.

FOOD

Once you've planned your route, you'll know how many meals will be eaten in the field. With this information in hand, you are ready to select your food. Before you start gathering the groceries, however, there are a few things to consider about winter menus.

Calorie Drain

The average, sedentary citizen, depending on age, occupation, and habits, can develop a roll around the waist on 2,300 to 2,800 calories a day. An active cold-weather camper, on the trail, can easily burn up 5,000 a day. It's almost impossible to plan backpacking meals that will offer that many calories, but if you don't replace a good part of them, the net loss will cut into your stamina until you're weaker than a cup of boarding-house coffee.

So, in order to avoid energy loss and fatigue, the winter camper needs to plan a high-energy menu. Since he also is fighting weight, he needs to select foods with a good weight-to-calorie ratio — that is, low in weight and high in calories. Chocolate, for example, has an excellent ratio since it offers 100 to 150 calories an ounce.

An even better example is a Wilson's meat bar. It yields an average of more than 500 calories per three-ounce bar, or more than 165 calories per ounce. Moreover, it contains a good deal of fat, which is an important item in a winter diet. The flavor and grainy consistency hardly make these bars gourmet favorites, even when mixed with other foods, but they are the best energy food for the weight that I know of.

Flour, on the other hand, is a poor example. Eight ounces will provide about 200 calories, or 25 calories per ounce. Flour is also bulky. It takes nearly a pound of it to make pancakes for two. So, while fresh bread and hotcakes are fine eating in the back country, they are too heavy to include on any but the shortest trips.

Variety and Fill

In addition to high calorie count, the winter camper's menu should provide good taste and variety. It's no accident that freeze-dried meals carry exotic names like turkey tetrazzini, beef stroganoff and chicken supreme. After that first day or so on the trail, it takes a highly seasoned dish to stimulate appetites dulled by fatigue. But once you've hardened to the trail, your appetite will become voracious. For this reason, many freeze-dried foods are based on some type of filler, such as rice, noodles, or macaroni. The idea is to provide that pleasant, belly-full feeling. This keeps you from braining your partner with a ski pole in a hassle over the last spoonful of beef stew.

Freeze-dried Foods

Nothing has eased the burden of the camper who carries his food with him more than our modern, space-age foods. These freeze-dried products have done much to eliminate problems of menu planning and cooking, too.

When we first started backpacking, my partner and I spent a

Typical selection of freeze-dried foods found at a local sporting goods store. (Photo courtesy of Milt McLaskey and Dana Van Burgh)

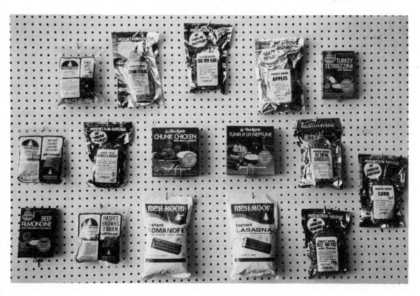

day before each trip carefully weighing and measuring foods from our bulk supplies. It was difficult to get variety and sufficient calories, yet stay within our weight limits. Today, it can be as simple as throwing a selection of prepackaged, freeze-dried meals into your pack.

These foods are sold by most camping suppliers. Some brands also are distributed through sporting goods outlets, and a few are even available from supermarkets.

While some freeze-dried foods require cooking and some need a little simmering, many can be prepared by merely adding cold or boiling water. Some brands can be prepared in their own container. With few exceptions, the packages and bags can be burned completely or reduced to a small bit of foil that can be carried out in your pack. Complete breakfast, lunch, and dinner menus come neatly packaged in one bag, usually in two- and four-man servings. These are the ultimate in convenience for the backpacker and the easy way out for many campers.

Personally, I never use the complete meal packages. I prefer to select my own menus. Besides, some lunch and most dinner meals include one and sometimes two vegetables. With the exception of dehydrated potatoes, I won't give a vegetable pack space, especially in wintertime. Producers like to point out that these complete menus are well balanced, which they no doubt are. However, winter pack trips are generally short and nutrition is of much less concern than energy and taste.

Fortunately, for those of us who like to exercise personal choice, most freeze-dried items are available in separate bags — again, usually in two- and four-man servings. They offer everything from beef steak to cottage cheese and cabbage to blueberry cobbler.

In selecting freeze-dried foods, you'll want to look for ease of preparation, fill quantity, and, of course, taste. Over the years, I've tried a variety of brands, most of them were reasonably good. There are, however, two brands that I've found to be generally excellent. Though taste may be a personal thing, most packers I know agree that these two products are "good tasting." They are Rich-Moor Foods and the Tea Kettle and Mountain House brands of Oregon Freeze-Dried Products.

For taste, Tea Kettle dinners are by far the best. They are gourmet quality and are very easily prepared by adding a small amount of boiling water to the container. Packaging is inconvenient, though it does provide a dish to use for other meals. They are somewhat expensive since servings are scanty. Even using a two-man portion for one camper yields a light meal, but supplemented with soup and dessert, they make an excellent dinner entree.

Rich-Moor is the best tasting of all the other brands I've tried. More importantly, the servings are the most generous. With all other products I've tried, the dinner meals, at least, must be doubled to feed a hungry camper. This isn't necessary with Rich-Moor dinners. The cooking of some items isn't as convenient as it might be, but that's not as important as generous portions and good taste.

Mountain House products are also good tasting and are, with the exception of their sister Tea Kettle brand, the most convenient to prepare. Most meals can be fixed in their own package by merely adding boiling water. Breakfast and lunch servings are adequate, but dinner portions have to be doubled.

I use other brands for some items, such as Wilson's steaks, hamburgers, and meat bars, and Trail Chef salads. And because freeze-dried foods are expensive, I also supplement from the supermarket shelf.

Supermarket Foods

Condensed and dehydrated foods can be purchased from the local supermarket in bulk and packaged at home. In fact, an entire trip menu could be selected from your local store; while it would be cheaper, it would mean a considerable increase in bulk and weight in your pack, as well as more cooking time and effort in the field.

Cereals (both hot and cold), dried soups, instant rice,

A typical selection of supermarket foods that can be packaged at home, which can mean a considerable savings. (Photo by Ray Stebbins)

noodles, powdered potatoes, powdered milk, Tang, fruit drinks, and powdered chocolate drinks are examples of items you can buy in bulk and package at home.

Items that don't need re-packaging include tubes of cheese, honey in plastic bottles, hard sausage, and a host of powdered gravies and flavorings. The latter run the gamut from hollandaise sauce to beef stroganoff mix. They can be used to make your own prepackaged dinners by adding them, along with some freeze-dried meat, to rice or noodles.

Breakfast setup of freeze-dried foods includes coffee, Tang (in plastic sack), hot cocoa mix, sausage patties, and scrambled eggs. The sausage patties, incidentally, are excellent. (Photo by Ray Stebbins)

Menu Planning

Choosing Food. Choice of food is a personal thing and no two campers ever fully agree on selections, so every trip will mean some compromise. Matters of taste must also give way to considerations of bulk and weight. In any case, each member of the group should have some say in menu planning. Foods for cold-weather camping should be selected with both weight and calories in mind. A sample five-day menu follows. Weights given are net. Container weight is estimated later.

FIRST DAY

Breakfast		Lunch	
Coffee			
Orange juice	3.0 oz.	Chicken salad	3.5 oz.
Cheese omelette	4.0 oz.	Trail crackers	4.0 oz.
Potatoes O'Brien	4.0 oz.	Hot lemonade	3.0 oz.
Bacon bar	3.0 oz.	Chocolate candy	4.0 oz.
	14.0 oz.		14.5 oz.

Dinner	
Beef bouillon	1.0 oz.
Beef steak	4.0 oz.
Instant potatoes	4.0 oz.
Powdered gravy	1.0 oz.
Pudding	10.0 oz.
	20.0 oz.

Total First Day: 48.5 oz.

On the above menu, all of the meats (except the hard sausage), the salads, the hash browns, egg dishes, and the dinner entrees are freeze-dried. These are left in their original containers. Items purchased from the supermarket, such as instant potatoes, bouillon cubes, Tang, and oatmeal, are measured out and weighed on a postal scale. Then they are packaged in doubled, plastic freezer bags and the tops are closed with rubber bands. Don't use the twist wires that are usually furnished, because they will poke holes in the other sacks.

For added convenience, we collect all of the items for one meal, put them together in a larger plastic sack, and mark them

SECOND DAY

Breakfast		Lunch	
Coffee			
Orange Tang (hot)	3.0 oz.		
Instant oatmeal			
(with sugar, milk		Cheese, fresh	4.0 oz.
& spices)	8.0 oz.	Trail crackers	4.0 oz.
Sausage patties	4.6 oz.	Ice cream	2.5 oz.
Hot chocolate	2.0 oz.	Beef bouillon	1.0 oz.
	17.6 oz.		11.5 oz.

Dinner

Pea soup	4.0 oz.
Beef Almondine	4.0 oz.
Chocolate cream pie	12.5 oz.
Coffee	
	20.5 oz.

Total Second Day: 49.6 oz.

as to type of meal and day, such as, "breakfast no. 1," or "dinner no. 5," and so on. This greatly simplifies packing and is a real timesaver in the field.

Planning for Weight. In checking the total weights of the above five-day, two-man menu, you can see that the total is fifteen pounds and three ounces, or a pound and a half per day, per man. However, that isn't quite all of it. You will note that no weight was given for coffee. That's because we carry 6 ounces of freeze-dried instant in a separate bag; this provides nearly 40 cups. We also take a plastic bottle of liquid oleo for use as cooking oil and as a substitute for butter. We pour a little out so that the container and contents weigh no more than 16 ounces.

THIRD DAY

Breakfast		Lunch	
Coffee			
Scrambled eggs			
and butter	2.5 oz.		
Hash brown potatoes		Hard sausage	4.0 oz.
and catsup	4.5 oz.	Trail crackers	4.0 oz.
Diced ham	2.0 oz.	Hot Jell-O	6.0 oz.
Hot chocolate	2.0 oz.	Candy	2.0 oz.
	11.0 oz.		16.0 oz.

Dinner	
Chili mac w/beef	10.1 oz.
Refried beans &	
cheese	6.0 oz.
French onion soup	2.0 oz.
Chocolate candy	2.0 oz.
	20.1 oz.

Total Third Day: 47.1 oz.

For trail snacks, we include a full pound of gorp. Gorp is a high energy mix of nuts, candies, and dried fruits in any combination you prefer. We generally take a mix of peanuts, chocolate bits, and raisins. Finally, with this menu, we take four ounces of extra catsup for the hash browns and four ounces of extra mayonnaise for the salads. All of this adds three pounds to our total food weight. When you figure in the weight of the containers, the grand total will hit about 19 pounds or nine and a half pounds per man to carry.

Check on Cooking Gear. In addition to controlling weight, a detailed menu serves as a check on cooking gear. You'll remember that our basic equipment consists of two pots, a

FOURTH DAY

Breakfast		Lunch	
Coffee			
Grapefruit Tang (hot)	3.0 oz.		
Instant oatmeal (with milk, sugar & apples)	8.0 oz.	Tuna salad	4.0 oz.
		Trail crackers	4.0 oz.
Sausage patties	4.6 oz.	Candy	2.0 oz.
Hot chocolate	2.0 oz.	Hot lemonade	3.0 oz.
	17.6 oz.		13.0 oz.

Dinner	
Ox tail soup	4.5 oz.
Turkey Tetrazzini	4.0 oz.
Cheese cake	10.5 oz.
	19.0 oz.

Total Fourth Day: 49.6 oz.

frying pan, and a cup, plate, fork, and spoon each. By visualizing how we will prepare each meal, we can determine if this is enough gear.

On the first day, at breakfast, we will use the two pots to make coffee and orange juice. When they have been consumed, water is heated in both pots for the eggs and potatoes. If we are using a single burner stove rather than an open fire, then only one pot can be heated at a time. In this case, we use the first pot of boiling water for the potatoes. Since they are freeze-dried, we merely dump them in the boiling water and set them aside to soak. The second pot is put on to boil, usually with extra water for more coffee. When it's hot, two cups of coffee are

FIFTH DAY

Breakfast		Lunch	
Coffee			
Orange Tang (hot)	3.0 oz.		
Western omelette	4.5 oz.	Chicken bouillon	1.0 oz.
Hash brown potatoes		Cheese spread	4.0 oz.
(with catsup)	4.5 oz.	Trail crackers	4.0 oz.
Pork patties	4.0 oz.	Ice cream	2.8 oz.
	16.0 oz.		11.8 oz.

Dinner	
Grapefruit Tang	
(hot)	3.0 oz.
Beef Stroganoff	
(with noodles)	10.5 oz.
Cottage cheese	2.1 oz.
Candy	2.0 oz.
	17.6 oz.

Total Fifth Day: 45.4 oz.

poured out and the eggs, also freeze-dried, are poured into the remaining water and set aside.

Meantime, the potatoes are drained and put in the frying pan with plenty of liquid oleo. The potatoes are browned while the eggs soak. When the hash browns are ready, we divide them up on our plates (heated, if there is an open fire). Then the eggs are drained and quickly heated before serving. The bacon bar is divided in half and eaten along with the eggs and potatoes.

At lunch, the salad is prepared in its own container with cold water, so we will need only one pot to heat the lemonade.

In preparing dinner, we will make the pudding first, but the pot we use will be needed to make the rest of the meal. Therefore we need some place to put the pudding. We could, of course, throw in an extra pot with our cook gear for this purpose. However, our menu indicates that pie is planned for two meals. So, instead, we'll take an eight-inch, aluminum pie plate. It will hold the pudding and also serve later for making the pies.

While the pudding is being prepared, water is boiling for the bouillon, which we will make in our drinking cups. When this is done, the steaks (freeze-dried and already cooked) are set to soaking in the pot used for bouillon. When the pudding pot is cleaned, it is used to prepare the instant mashed potatoes. When the steaks are thoroughly soaked, they are drained and put in the frying pan. The gravy is made in the water used to soak the steaks. Then the steaks and gravy are heated together in the frying pan, the potatoes are warmed and dinner is ready.

By a similar check of each day's menu, we can quickly determine if any other additional cooking gear will be required.

CHECK LIST

With food checked and packaged and the rest of your equipment gathered, you are ready to load up for a trip. First, however, you'll need to prepare a check list. This is a very necessary chore, since it is the only means of being certain that you are not leaving behind something essential.

In the early 1800s, French-Canadian trappers often made what they called a Hudson Bay start. On the first day, they traveled only a very short distance from the fort or trading post. Then, by going through their regular camp routine, they quickly discovered if they had left something behind. If they had, it was an easy matter to return the short distance to the fort and retrieve it.

Though a real Hudson Bay start is inefficient in these modern days, taking one mentally is a good way to formulate a check list. In your mind, go through your camping routine for a

Food and equipment set out and ready to be ticked off the checklist. (Photo by Ray Stebbins)

full day. Visualize leaving your jump-off point, traveling, preparing meals, setting up camp, dressing and sleeping. Jot down the equipment required as you go through each step. For the first trip or so, you will probably want to check your own list against one that has actually been used. Here's an example of one from a recent trip.

BASIC EQUIPMENT

Backpack	3 lb.	
Sleeping bag & stuff sack	5 lb.	
Sleeping pad	1 lb.	
Tent (Warmlite) poles & pegs	3 lb.	5 oz.
Total Basic Equipment Weight	12 lb.	5 oz.

CLOTHING (in pack)

Extra socks (two pair)		8 oz.
Extra felt liners		14 oz.
Extra cotton longjohns	1 lb.	
Wool shirt		15 oz.
Down shirt	1 lb.	4 oz.
Wet gear (chaps & jacket)	1 lb.	
Quilted underwear	1 lb.	
Total Clothing Weight	6 lb.	9 oz.

COOKING GEAR (2 man)

Stove (partner carries fuel can)   2 lb.
2 pots
1 fry pan
2 cups
2 forks
2 spoons
3 plates
1 packet matches
1 combo salt & pepper shaker
1 grill (if open fires
   are planned)
1 bit of plastic scrubber
4 plastic bags

Total Weight of Cook Gear 3 lb.   (one man) 1 lb. 8 oz.

TOILET KIT

1 roll paper
Toothbrush
Small tube toothpaste
Small soap
1 Handiwipe

Total Weight of Kit   12 oz.

FIRST AID KIT

2 compresses
1 roll gauze
1 roll tape
1 plastic tube pain pills
1 plastic tube halazone tablets
1 tube sun screen ointment

Total Weight of Kit   12 oz.

MISCELLANEOUS

Goggles w/extra lenses	8 oz.
50-foot nylon parachute cord	4 oz.
Folding saw	8 oz.
Thermometer w/case	1 oz.
Compass & 2 USGS maps	6 oz.
Aluminum bottle (1 quart)	5 oz.
Plastic trowel	8 oz.
Notebook & pencil	2 oz.
Fire kit	
matches	
starter	
tinder	3 oz.
Extra matches (2 packs in plastic)	1 oz.
Total Miscellaneous Gear	2 lb. 14 oz.
Total Equipment in Pack	26 lb. 12 oz.
Food for Five Days (per packer)	9 lb. 8 oz.
Total Pack Weight for Five-Day Trip	36 lb. 4 oz.

TO WEAR AND CARRY IN POCKETS

Net underwear
Cotton longjohns
Wool shirt
Wool pants
Blanket-weight wool jacket
Windproof parka
Wool hat & combination face mask
Belt
Belt knife
Pocket knife
Mallory flashlight
Gaiters
Socks, liners and boots
Fire kit
Extra compass
Gloves
Packet of gorp

TRAVEL GEAR (optional)

Snowshoes
Bindings
Skis
Waxes, cork, scraper
Ski poles
Cover for ski boots

Completed pack, checked and ready for the trail. (Photo by Ray Stebbins)

In using this or any other packing list, it is essential that no item be checked off until it is actually put in the pack, in your pocket, on your back, or in the vehicle.

ALCOHOL

You will note that no provision is made in the food or pack list for alcoholic drinks. In summer, I always pack a jug and cocktail hour is a pleasant part of the camping routine. In winter, however, I generally leave it at home because of its dehydrating effect on the system. If you do take alcohol in cold weather, take it easy and drink plenty of water to offset its drying effect. Incidentally, *never* carry your booze in a soft plastic container — use aluminum bottles or tin flasks.

LOADING

When loading a contour frame pack for use in hiking or snowshoeing, you'll want to keep the weightiest objects high and close to the back. Think of the pack as divided into three zones: zone A, the triangular section high and next to the back, where the heaviest items would be loaded; zone B, the middle section where the next heaviest gear would go, with the weightier items toward the top of the zone; and zone C, farthest from the packer's back for the lightest gear.

If you are loading a skier's packsack or a contour to be used by a skier, you will have the same three zones. This time, however, the A zone triangle would be on the bottom, nearest the back. The heavier items will still be loaded in zone A, but the weighty gear will go toward the bottom of the pack rather than the top.

Once your pack is loaded and the check list completed, you can adjust the shoulder straps and balance the load. Dress in the shirts and jackets you will wear on the trail, then slip into your pack. Shrug up your shoulders and tighten the hip belt so that most of the weight is supported on the hips. Now, adjust the shoulder straps so that the pack is snug against your back. Then walk around for a few minutes to see if one side of the pack seems heavier than the other. If it does, rearrange items in the load until it feels balanced. This should do it, though you may want to make some adjustments after the first half hour or so on the trail.

PACK WEIGHT

A pack that is too heavy can spoil your trip. The basic rule to

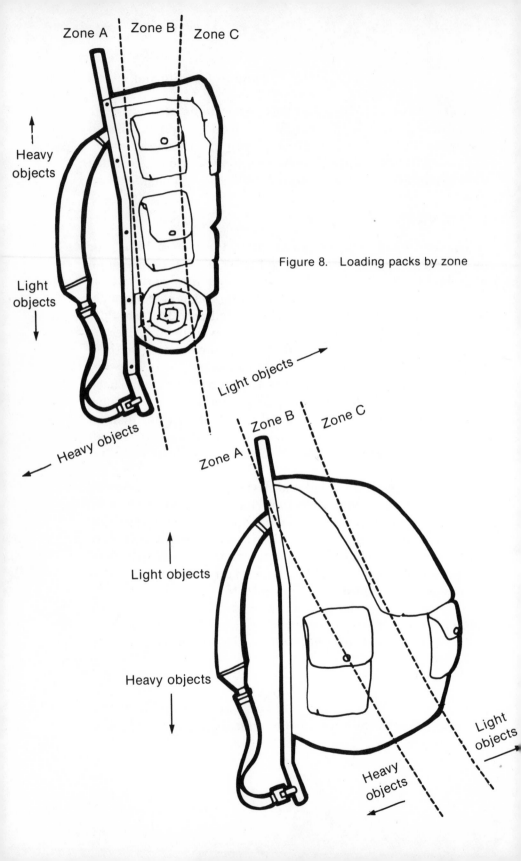

Figure 8. Loading packs by zone

remember is that a forty-pound pack is not five pounds heavier than a thirty-five-pound pack; it is twice as heavy. Of course, a forty-five-pound pack is twice as heavy as a forty-pounder.

You'll notice that with the check list given above, individual weights are given for most items. This is because I like to keep a record as I load. You can, however, weigh the completed pack on your bathroom scales.

In winter, I try to keep the total weight of basic equipment around twenty-five pounds. This leaves ten pounds for food, to keep the pack weight at a reasonable thirty-five pounds. Actually, mine runs a little heavier since I take camera gear and often some fishing equipment. Still, I try to hold the weight at forty pounds for a five-day trip. And, for me, forty-five heavy ones constitute the absolute maximum. If you can stay close to thirty-five, you'll enjoy it more. Among a group of packers, weight loads should be equalized as much as possible.

WEATHER

You should also check predicted weather conditions when you are planning your winter camping trip. Light snowstorms are no problem; in fact, most winter campers soon come to look on snow as friendly. However, you do have one dangerous enemy in cold weather — the wind. It has, in fact, so significant an effect on safety that there is an old mountaineer's slogan, "Travel in snow; in wind, don't go." The wind can drastically lower the actual temperatures. This effect, known as the wind chill factor, is discussed more fully in the following chapter.

By checking the past records of average monthly temperatures and precipitation, you can get an idea of which winter months offer the best chance for good weather. It is also a good idea to make a last minute check on the weather. You'll want to know about any major storm that may be moving into the area. If your local station predicts severe weather, stay home. They might be wrong, but it doesn't make sense to risk a trip that could be both miserable and dangerous.

Campers starting out on a trip. (Photo by Ray Stebbins)

4

How to Enjoy It

For those who have never tried it, cold-weather camping may seem like an advanced exercise for Boy Scouts or a maneuver for male masochists. Not so. It can be a challenge, of course, but it's *fun*. However, the enjoyment is lost if you get cold, hungry, or exhausted. This chapter deals with techniques that will help make your camping enjoyable.

WIND AND WEATHER

It is important to pay close attention to weather reports and to note wind speed as well as the still air temperature. The combination of wind and low temperature can be deadly. If you know the still air temperature and the wind speed, you can use the Wind Chill Chart to determine the effective temperature — the one you feel.

In general terms, a well-dressed camper will be comfortable in temperatures down to -20 degrees F. When the wind chill factor is between -30 and -40 degrees F., it can be both

WIND CHILL CHART

Estimated Wind Speed in MPH	Actual Thermometer Reading (°F.)											
	50	40	30	20	10	0	-10	-20	-30	-40	-50	-60
	Equivalent Temperature (°F.)											
Calm	50	40	30	20	10	0	-10	-20	-30	-40	-50	-60
5	48	37	27	16	6	-5	-15	-26	-36	-47	-57	-68
10	40	28	16	4	-9	-21	-33	-46	-58	-70	-83	-95
15	36	22	9	-5	-18	-36	-45	-58	-72	-85	-99	-112
20	32	18	4	-10	-25	-39	-53	-67	-82	-96	-110	-124
25	30	16	0	-15	-29	-44	-59	-74	-88	-104	-118	-133
30	28	13	-2	-18	-33	-48	-63	-79	-94	-109	-125	-140
35	27	11	-4	-20	-35	-49	-67	-82	-98	-113	-129	-145
40	26	10	-6	-21	-37	-53	-69	-85	-100	-116	-132	-148

(wind speeds greater than 40 mph have little addi-tional effect)

LITTLE DANGER

(for properly clothed person)

INCREASING DANGER

GREAT DANGER

(danger from freezing of exposed flesh)

uncomfortable and hazardous. This is a good time to stay close to a warming fire. A wind of twenty miles per hour with a still air temperature of -20 degrees F. produces an effective wind chill temperature of -68 degrees F. This is a point at which any exposed flesh will freeze in approximately one minute. When temperatures are in that range, it's a good time to stay home.

To sum up, in moderate winds of ten to twenty miles per hour, it is only safe to travel if the still air temperature is no lower than zero degrees F. In the case of heavy winds, thirty to forty miles per hour, the minimum safe temperature is ten degrees above zero.

Incidentally, if you keep your thermometer in an outside pocket of your pack rather than your shirt pocket, you can check temperatures more quickly. You won't have to wait for it to drop down from ninety-eight degrees.

ORIENTATION

With wind and weather right, you are ready to move out. As soon as you are away from the vehicles so that they won't affect the compass, stop and orient yourself with the map. Align it with magnetic north, using the declination arrow on the map, as described in chapter 3. Study the terrain, noting any major landmarks and comparing map contours with what you can see. Review your route, which should be drawn on the map, and note any features such as lakes, streams, or peaks that will be along your trail. All members of the group should share in the procedure so that everyone understands the route.

Once you have strapped on your packs and have started up the trail, keep your compass handy to check your line of travel. A map and compass are worthless unless they are used, don't be shy about consulting them. Getting lost in summer is no fun; in winter it can be disastrous.

STAYING WARM

Obviously, in order to enjoy winter camping, you must stay

warm. In the northern United States and southern Canada, the wintertime temperatures are often above zero, but they can drop to thirty or forty below for days at a time. Yet the truth is, it's easier to stay warm in severe cold than to remain cool in very hot weather.

I have camped in tropical heat on the banks of the Orinoco River in Venezuela. The climate was so enervating that after a few days I found myself exhausted by the slightest physical effort. On the other hand, scientists at arctic bases manage to work efficiently at -70 degrees F. and lower.

The body itself is an efficient producer of heat and is the main source of warmth for the winter camper. In order to keep up with increased demands for both energy and heat, caused by cold weather, the body reacts by increasing its metabolic rate. This boost in the rate at which food is converted into energy and heat requires a corresponding increase in the amount of calories we consume. So, in addition to three hearty meals a day, it is important to keep plenty of high energy snacks handy to munch at trail breaks and in camp. Cold-weather camping, in fact, should be a glutton's delight, since it's necessary to eat constantly to stay warm.

The body's circulation must not be impaired in any way, if it is to operate as an efficient heating device. Clothing, with the exception of cuffs and gaiters, should be loose with no binding or tightness anywhere. Nor should boots be laced so tightly that they restrict circulation. It should be pointed out here that the best way to keep the feet warm is to keep the rest of the body well covered. If your toes feel cold, it may be that you need more clothes on your back. The old Swede was right when he said, "If your feet are cold, put on your hat."

The heat produced by the body must not be allowed to dissipate into the cold air around us. Or rather, the rate at which it dissipates must be controlled. We do this, of course, with our layers of clothing. The insulating quality of what we wear and the warmth it affords can be greatly impaired by both wind and wetness.

Your parka, hat, gloves, and face mask will be sufficient

protection in moderate winds. In the case of high winds, you simply get off the trail and wait it out under shelter.

Wetness can be more or less of a problem, depending on the type of cold encountered. In Alaska and northern Canada, winter brings dry cold. This means that during the day, temperatures will remain well below freezing. Since there is no melting, you don't have much opportunity to get wet.

In the northern U.S. and southern Canada, however, especially in spring and fall, the cold-weather camper will be fighting wet cold. That is, temperatures will be above freezing at some time during the day, and some melting will occur. Under these conditions, it is difficult to stay dry. Wet snow is sticky snow. It clings to pants, jackets and boots. At every step, the weeds and bushes slap it on your clothing. You brush it from the rocks, and, in the woods, it drops from the trees, splattering over your head and shoulders in a shower of freezing slush. It then melts quickly, wetting everything to which it has stuck.

Wearing a windproof parka will help since snow won't cling to its smooth surface as easily as it will to a fluffy material like wool. But in most cases, it won't be enough to keep you dry. You'll have to dig out your wet gear. Remember though, to shed some clothing and to slow your pace in order to avoid excessive sweating.

If you are wearing leather boots, the wet cold can give you trouble. No matter how well you've treated them with silicone or grease, boots won't stay dry for more than a day in slushy snow. The skier hasn't much choice, but the hiker or snow-shoer can wear paks or rubber boots to keep his feet dry. The rubber boots will sweat more and your socks will get wet from the inside. But it's easier to dry socks wet from perspiration than those soaked with water.

In good weather, you can hang your socks on your pack to dry. On bad days, put them inside your shirt, flat against your belly. Cold, wet feet are an invitation to frostbite, and it is essential to have extra dry socks so that a pair is available for changing when you reach a campsite.

During the day, you can dry socks by hanging them on your pack. (Photo by Ray Stebbins)

Staying warm also means staying dry from the inside as well as out. Clothing soaked by perspiration does not provide effective insulation against the cold and can lead to severe chilling. The easiest way to avoid excessive sweating is to adjust your clothing. The great advantage of the layer system is that you can peel off whatever it takes to keep you cool.

Sometimes it is enough to merely remove a hat or gloves, unbutton a collar, or roll up your sleeves, for exposing a portion of bare skin to the cooling action of the air may be enough to cool the entire body.

Some perspiring, of course, in unavoidable and, in fact, is essential for regulating body temperature. In the cold of winter, however, the camper who doesn't sweat excessively is often unaware that he is losing body fluid. Under no compulsion to replace it, he may allow himself to become dehydrated. This seriously impairs the heat producing capabilities of the body. In severe cases, dehydration can lead to exhaustion and is often a contributing factor in death from exposure.

It is extremely important, therefore, that the winter camper drink fluids as often as possible. Routes should be planned along streams or lakes whenever feasible. Breaking through the ice to obtain water saves fuel and is much more efficient than melting snow.

If there is no water along the trail, you can eat snow (never ice). Just be certain that you melt and warm it in your mouth before swallowing. This will keep your mouth from drying out

It's important to adjust your clothing to keep from overheating on the trail.
(Photo by Ray Stebbins)

and prevent chilling of the stomach. At the noon break, drink at least a pint of fluid, and more, if possible, at dinner.

So staying warm isn't merely a matter of the right amount of proper clothing. It is a combination of little things that add up to a basic plan: 1) eat well and often; 2) wear loose clothing; 3) protect yourself from the wind; 4) keep dry; 5) avoid excessive sweating; and 6) drink plenty of fluids.

FIGHTING FATIGUE

Preventing exhaustion is nearly as important to successful winter camping as staying warm. Normally, the winter camper will expend more energy than his summer counterpart. It takes a good bit of energy just to keep warm in cold weather. And the winter sportsman is usually engaged in strenuous activity — hiking, snowshoeing, or skiing in rugged terrain — as well. Even snowmobiling takes a lot of energy, as anyone who has ridden mountain trails or dug his machine from a bank of rotten snow will tell you. Therefore, it is important to guard against becoming overtired.

Fortunately, many of the things we do to keep warm such as eating high energy foods, drinking fluids, staying dry and keeping out of the wind, also help prevent fatigue. The winter camper can also harbor energy by learning to pace himself.

Pacing

A useful technique in summer and an essential one in winter, pacing requires the acceptance of one basic rule: *Always match your pace to your breathing, never your breathing to your pace.* This is especially important for those over forty. Properly done, pacing enables a camper in good condition to climb steep grades steadily without losing his breath or increasing his heart rate beyond sensible limits. As a result, pacing prevents excessive perspiration and greatly reduces fatigue.

The technique is simple. While maintaining the same steady rhythm of deep breathing, vary your pace to suit the terrain.

For example, on smooth, level ground, you might take two or three steps with snowshoes or several glides with skis to one complete breathing cycle. On moderate slopes, you would reduce your pace, taking only one or two steps, or glides, in one breathing cycle. On very steep grades, you might take only half a step as you slowly inhale and exhale. The important thing is to set your own rhythm of deep breathing and maintain it regardless of pace or terrain. Once you have developed this deep breathing as a habit, you'll find it not only fights fatigue, but it also takes all the hassle out of steep climbs.

Since everyone has his own optimum rate of speed, it's best not to try and match your pace to that of someone else. Few chores are more tiring than trying to keep up with a speeder or holding back for a creeper. The ideal is to let everyone set his own pace, while making certain that the group doesn't get too spread out. On the trail in winter, a group should keep each other in sight at all times.

If anyone is so slow as to seriously delay the trip, he should, of course, be encouraged to speed up. Placing him in the lead will often stimulate him to a faster pace. This problem can be avoided, however, if you know your partners' hiking habits before you accept him as a winter companion.

Other Tips

If your group is traveling through deep snow, it is a good idea to rotate the lead. Breaking trail can wear a man down quickly.

Rest breaks should be taken every hour. Stop and get off your feet, if possible. This is a good time to have a snack and drink some water. Try to relax feet and leg muscles. Five minutes will be enough, but a break shouldn't be any less. The idea is not to rest because you *feel* tired, but so you *won't* feel tired.

Don't let yourself get pushed on the trail. With your tent to protect you from the wind, a stove, and snow to melt, you're independent enough to camp almost anywhere. So always

Trail breaks should be taken before you feel tired — at least one every hour. (Photo by Ray Stebbins)

stop for the day before you begin to feel tired. Going too fast and too far just to reach some preplanned objective is asking for trouble. Pushing yourself to the point of exhaustion can spoil a summer trip, in winter it can be fatal.

PITCHING CAMP

Winter days are short, so you don't want to travel too long into the afternoon. It's best to stop and make a camp at least two hours before sundown. This will provide about two and a half hours of usable light, time enough to set up a snug camp and to cook dinner.

If you are in mountainous country and there is heavy snow, a prime consideration for a campsite is that it be clear of snow slide or avalanche danger. The simple solution is to pick a flat spot in a wooded area. The first requirement is a sheltered location with plenty of firewood available. Then look for a stream or lake nearby. It saves both time and fuel to be able to get water without melting snow, or at least to have ice, which produces water more quickly.

Once camp is located, the next move is to pick a spot to pitch the tent. It should be in an area that is clear overhead, that is, free of any overhanging branches. Snow loads that accumulate on the branches, can fall at any time, smashing the tent and its occupants. Even if the trees are completely free of snow, avoid them. An unexpected storm could load them up during the night. Also, check the area for deadfall. High winds are common in winter and you don't want any dead trees lined up to blow down on your tent.

Using snowshoes, boots, or skis, stomp down and level an area a foot larger all-around than the floor area of your tent.

Wearing his pack to add weight, the author stamps down the snow with snowshoes to make a campsite. (Photo by Ray Stebbins)

Packing it hard will prevent the snow under your shelter from getting lumpy. It also helps to cut small evergreen boughs to lay on the snow beneath the tent. This will insulate against the cold and keep the floor from freezing to the snow. Some campers use a three mil plastic sheet for this purpose, but I don't like the added weight.

With your tent laid out, the staking may be done in several ways. If there is plenty of snow depth, pegs can be improvised from sticks a foot or more long and about finger thick. Placed through the peg loops and thrust deeply into the snow, they will hold very well.

To use regular pegs, dig a hole in the snow with the heel of your boot where you want the peg to go. Pack snow into the hole and stomp it down solidly. When you have built up a hardpacked mound, drive the peg into it just as you would in the ground.

If there is no snow and the earth is frozen tight, deadfall can be used in place of pegs. Find two lengths of down timber three to four inches in diameter and long enough to extend several feet beyond your tent at both ends. Lay them along each side of the shelter and tie the peg loops to them. If needed, use two shorter logs, stuck under the ends of the long ones, to tie down front and back guy ropes.

As soon as the tent is up, place your foam pad and sleeping bag inside and roll them out. The bag should be well fluffed so that it fills with air.

To keep everything drier, it helps to stomp down the snow in the immediate camp area. If you plan an open fire, the area around the fireplace should be packed especially hard. Also, beat down any paths you will be using to go for wood or water. When camp is secure, it's time to brush off your boots and dry them on the outside as well as possible. Then, before tackling the chores of making fire and dinner, change socks and replace any items of wet clothing with something dry.

FIRES AND COOKING

The open campfire is currently the subject of much

controversy. One of my favorite camping partners, David Sumner, an ardent outdoorsman, roundly condemns open fires. Dave remains convinced that those sputtering little blowtorches with names like Optimus and Primus are all the warmth and comfort a man needs in his winter camp. Objecting first of all that making a fire is too much trouble, he complains more seriously that collecting firewood destroys the pristine nature of the woods — that too many trees have been brutally scarred by eager campers in their never ending search for fuel. He says the end result will be millions of acres of ruined and denuded forests.

I suppose Dave is right and the day is coming when hordes of campers will have burned up the tons of deadfall that fill our forests. But though it would be difficult, and at times impossible, to camp without those little gas stoves, I'd be sad to think that I had only those smelly, stuttering little contraptions to cheer my winter camp. For me, the true mystique of the outdoors is found in the deeply primitive relationship between man and weather, man and sun, man and fire. Without a campfire, an essential element in that relationship is gone.

Fire Building

Moreover, we are referring to an outdoorsman's fire and not the huge, useless bonfire of the beginning camper. The cooking fire of the experienced woodsman is small. Its fuel is squaw wood, short sticks no larger than the thickness of your thumb. And the fire is never any bigger than the pot or pots it has to heat.

And, despite Dave's objections, building a fire in winter isn't that much work. Snow on the ground is only a minor complication. If it isn't too deep, you can dig, scoop, or scrape it away and build your fire on the ground. In deep snow, you may be able to find a rock or boulder outcrop that will make a good base. Even making your fire on the snow doesn't pose much of a problem. Cut four or five green logs about four inches in diameter and some two feet long. Lay them on the snow to

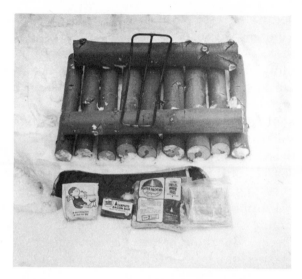

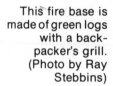
This fire base is made of green logs with a backpacker's grill. (Photo by Ray Stebbins)

make a platform and build your fire on it. This green wood base will last for several meals.

If green wood isn't available, deadfall can be used, but it will require more logs. Lay four or five on the snow, then, alternating direction, place another layer crosswise to the

This fire base is set up with layers of cut deadfall. Squaw wood is ready along with extra logs for building up the base when needed. A spit is set up to hold pots. (Photo by Ray Stebbins)

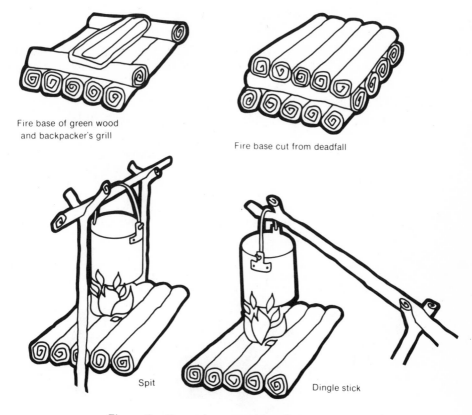

Fire base of green wood
and backpacker's grill

Fire base cut from deadfall

Spit

Dingle stick

Figure 9.   Preparing a cooking fire

first and alternate again with a third row. When you make your fire on this platform, it sinks into the logs instead of the snow.

Before striking a match, you'll want to have plenty of firewood within handy reach. And you shouldn't have to mutilate live trees to get it. In nearly all of the back country of Canada and the U.S., there is plenty of standing, dead timber to use for firewood. Also, on many living evergreens, there are dead branches on the lower part of the trunk that make excellent kindling. In most cases, you won't need any cutting tools, since wood for a cooking fire needn't be any larger than those dead branches that can be broken off by hand.

In winter, it often happens that firewood is damp from snow

or storm. Yet, you can usually find dry tinder by breaking off the small, tangled twigs that curl under the heavier limbs of the spruce and fir. Or, you can whittle long, thin chips from the dry insides of larger branches. Dead evergreen needles make excellent tinder, since they are practically waterproof and will always burn with a quick, hot flame. Of course, with fire starter, a butane lighter or a candle, you can light even wet tinder.

To start your fire, cover some tinder with a small tepee of match-sized kindling. Over it build another tepee of slightly larger, pencil-sized sticks. Light these, and once they are burning, you can add slightly bigger sticks, even if they are damp. Once the fire is going, stack your damp firewood on the smoky side of the fireplace to dry out.

Here the author used fire starter to light a tepee pile of kindling. (Photo by Ray Stebbins)

Cooking

Once your fire is going, the next step is to use it. For convenience, I often carry a seven-ounce backpacker's grill. Set over the fire, on green logs or rocks, it will hold two pots. If pack weight is running heavy, however, and it often does in cold weather, I'll leave the grill at home and improvise a spit or dingle stick.

A spit is two forked sticks, stuck in the snow on each side of the fire with another stick placed in the forks to form a cross piece. You can hang a pair of pots from the cross piece. A dingle stick is a straight branch, stuck in the snow at an angle, supported in the middle by a rock or another stick, and positioned so that its upper end is over the fire. It will hold a single pot.

If the area you are in prohibits open fires, or if there is no firewood easily available, you may want to use your gasoline stove. If you plan to use it outside, you may have to devise some kind of wind shield. A strong breeze won't blow out the flame, but it will carry away much of the heat. Most stoves are provided with wind guards, but they are generally ineffective. However, a log, a few rocks or mound of snow will take care of the problem. You'll also need to build a small platform of squaw wood to set the stove on; otherwise, it will melt itself into a hole.

One solution to cooking in bad weather is to cook inside your tent. You'll still need some squaw wood insulation between the stove and the tent floor. Good ventilation is essential, since these little torches can burn up plenty of oxygen and can make a tent uncomfortably hot. And don't fill the stove's fuel tank inside the tent. Not only is there fire danger, but any spillage will leave stinking, eye-watering fumes that will last for hours. So, despite cold, storm, and inconvenience, it's best to fill the stove outside. And, don't forget to check the fuel container for leaks after using it. When the cap has been replaced, squeeze the can. Escaping air means that you haven't tightened it enough.

In bad weather, you can set up to cook inside your tent, but it's more fun to prepare meals outside over an open fire. (Photo by Ray Stebbins)

In cold weather, compact cookers, though advertised as self-priming or self-pressured, can be tricky to light. This includes my favorite backpacking stove, the Optimus 8R. Nearly all of these little gasoline stoves are primed in the same way. The fuel tank is pressured and, when a needle valve is cracked, gasoline flows into the priming bowl. The valve is closed and the gasoline is lighted. Its heat primes the stove's generator and when the generator is hot, the valve is reopened and the stove starts burning.

Larger models, such as the Optimus 111B, have finger pumps to pressure the fuel tank. The smaller types don't have this feature and are therefore called self-priming. Of course they are not. You, the operator, must do the job by providing the pressure to move the fuel from tank to priming bowl. This is generally done by simply warming the fuel tank in your hands. As your hands warm the air inside the tank, the air expands creating the pressure that will push the gasoline into the bowl when you open the valve.

Normally, it works rather well, but in very cold weather it is difficult to heat the air sufficiently with your hands alone. I have used a candle to supply the heat, but now Optimus has a priming paste that does the job. You put the paste in the priming bowl and light it. This furnishes the heat to start the generator and eliminates the problem of pressuring the tank. The paste also can be used as a fire starter. No matter what you do, your self-pressuring stove won't operate very well if you forget to let air into the tank before priming it. All you need do is remove and immediately replace the cap on the fuel tank. This assures you that there will be sufficient air in the container to expand and provide operating pressure.

Preparing Meals

Whether you are using a gasoline stove or an open fire, preparing freeze-dried or dehydrated foods is mostly a matter of boiling water. And since you are limited as to the amount of cook gear you can carry, making meals often becomes a game of musical pots. The most efficient cook is the one with the most hot water; as soon as one dish is finished, he grabs the pot it's in, cleans it, refills it, and sets it back on the fire.

At breakfast, for example, you might need water for nearly all of the following: juice crystals, coffee, hot chocolate, cereal, freeze-dried eggs, dehydrated potatoes, freeze-dried ham, more coffee, and dish water. Soon it gets to be a habit to keep water, or melting snow, on the fire always.

There is a trick to melting snow. Always start with a compressed ball in the bottom of the pot. Let it melt to cover the bottom with an inch or so of water before adding any more snow. If you scoop up a pot full and put it on the stove, the wicking action of the snow on top will absorb the water, leaving the bottom of the container dry. Of course, it's easy to burn a hole in a dry pot.

With all of the excellent prepackaged, freeze-dried foods available, you can prepare gourmet meals, even if you cook like Og-Son-Of-Fire. Simply follow the directions on the package. However, there are a few exceptions. When a product calls for soaking in water prior to cooking, you'll want to double the suggested time. Solid meats are particularly hard to re-hydrate. This includes the chunks of meat found in some salads, stews and pasta dishes. Also, at any altitude over 5,000 feet, it is usually necessary to extend the cooking time for most foods. And the higher you go, the longer it takes. So don't cook by time, but by taste.

Cleanup is easy in winter. The best way is to set the dirty dishes in the snow and let the food remnants freeze. Then, with a stick, scrape or chip out these remains and dunk the gear in boiling water. Soap is neither necessary nor desirable, since in cold weather its vestiges are likely to make you sick.

SLEEPING WARMLY

In addition to a satisfying meal, a good night's sleep is essential to the enjoyment of cold-weather camping. Staying warm during the night depends, to a great extent, on the design of your sleeping bag and tent as discussed in a previous chapter. However, here are a few hints that will help on those nights when the trees crack like rifle shots.

If you have cooked your evening meal inside, chances are that the tent has heated up considerably. Crawling into a heavy down bag in a warm tent is not only uncomfortable, it can cause heavy sweating. Later, when the air has cooled, the extra moisture in your bag will cause chilling. So, it's a good idea to open up and cool off the tent before you hit the sack.

Sleeping in the clothes you have worn all day also is a poor practice. They will be damp from perspiration and will make poor insulators. You'll end up much colder than if you had slept nude. It is better to have an extra pair of long underwear for sleeping. If you don't have any extra dry clothes, then you're better off sleeping bare.

Most cold-weather sleeping bags are equipped with a hood. If yours isn't, then it's a good idea to wear a wool stocking cap because if your head is cold, it's likely that the rest of you will be too. A pair of dry socks will warm your feet and you can shuck them off later. If you feel cold when you first crawl into the sack, a few dynamic tension exercises, which you can do without getting out of your bag, will warm you up.

You should also have food and water near you in the night. Keeping some high energy foods handy to munch on if you wake up is a mountaineer's trick. Along with the food, you'll want some water to drink. You could keep a pot of snow by your bunk, since water would freeze. A better way is to use left-over water from dinner or melt some snow and put it in your aluminum water bottle. Make sure the lid is tight, then take it into your sleeping bag, where it won't freeze.

These simple practices can mean the difference between a pleasant, warm night and a tense, wakeful one.

THAWING BOOTS

By the end of the day, leather boots are likely to be damp, if not wet, and you'll want to keep them from freezing during the night. Some campers take them into the sleeping bag with them, but I don't recommend this practice; it's likely to cause chilling. I prefer to wipe and dry the boots as well as possible and put them under the edge of my sleeping bag. Usually enough warmth will escape through the bag to keep them from turning into blocks of ice.

If they do freeze, thaw them very gently over a fire, being careful not to let the leather get hot. This should be done before

With fireplace laid and tent set up, you're ready for a cozy evening. (Photo by Ray Stebbins)

you put them on. Since feet are more tender in cold weather, the stiff boots could easily injure them.

SNOW LOAD

Even on cold nights, when sudden storms drop a light, powdery snow, the stuff can pile up on your tent and cause problems. Worst is the wet snow that sticks to the walls and roof of your shelter. As the weight of the snow increases, a tent peg may come out, or a rope give way, or the roof sag down on your face. You'll wake up with a start, a little spooked until you realize what's happening. Then you beat on the tent to knock off the snow and crawl out to replace a peg or rope, if necessary. It isn't dangerous, just annoying, but you should be prepared for it.

On your first night in a winter camp, you'll probably be tired and a little uneasy. Then, as you relax in the soft, warm down, listening to that special silence of the winter's night, you'll be glad you're there.

Campers in the high country. (Photo courtesy of Page Fagan)

5

How to Handle Trouble

It's possible that you may enjoy cold-weather camping for years and never have any real problems, since most of them can be avoided by using caution and common sense. Camping, after all, isn't like mountain climbing. The mountaineer accepts definite risks in order to accomplish his goal. The camper is merely out to have fun — he isn't called upon to take chances.

Yet it seems that there are times when any of us can become careless, forgetful, or mule-headed. And chances are that at least once during your confrontation with winter, you'll get caught by severe weather, encounter dangerous terrain, get lost, or have someone in your party injured. So, this chapter deals with trouble, how to avoid it, and when you can't, how to deal with it. (A section in Chapter 7 on survival skills also will tell you how to cope with extreme situations.)

DANGEROUS TERRAIN — AVALANCHES

For most winter campers, the mountains offer the ultimate in

The avalanche, though deadly, is nonetheless beautiful. (Photo courtesy of the U.S. Forest Service)

outdoor adventure. But while they undoubtedly provide the most scenic and challenging conditions, the mountains also present unique dangers. Of these, none is more impressive than the snow slide or avalanche. In seconds, it can send tons of snow roaring down the slopes at 180 miles an hour, blasting down everything in its path, including any unwary camper who happens to get in its way.

Once, in the process of trying to learn about snow slides, I spent two days with Den Davidson, a well-known pioneer in avalanche control. He was working for a Colorado mining company and his job was to trigger avalanches under controlled conditions. The idea was to bring them down without destroying company property or killing any personnel.

Den Davidson aims a gas cannon while his assistant, Rich Lane, observes. The gun uses gas pressure to fire an explosive charge into the starting zone of an avalanche to bring it down safely. (Photo by Ray Stebbins)

He and his assistant Rich Lane were quite successful. They used explosive charges that were propelled from a safe distance by a high pressure gas gun. Before the gun was developed, they used to ski the slopes, hand-throwing dynamite charges to set off the snow slides. The fact that they had survived was an indication of their knowledge of avalanche conditions.

During my visit, Davidson told me a great deal about snow hydrology and explained how they checked snow depth, took core samples, measured temperatures, and kept all kinds of records in an attempt to predict the behavior of snow slides. And in the course of this and other studies, some general conclusions have been reached. Generally speaking, the worst

This series of avalanche paths is named the Seven Sisters and is classified as an area of small but frequent slides. (Photo courtesy of the U.S. Forest Service)

time for avalanches is after a heavy snow, especially one accompanied by high winds or by wide variations in temperature. And though slides have come off slopes as slight as twenty degrees, the most dangerous areas are those thirty to forty degrees that have a dish-shaped profile. Den assured me, however, that the only reliable characteristic of the avalanche is its utter unpredictability.

Consequently, the average camper, in an effort to avoid the danger, won't get much help from a study of snow hydrology. His best shot is simply to avoid slide areas. The easiest way to do this is to stay in heavy timber and to cross only minor slopes of less than twenty degrees. Sometimes it is possible, and well worth the effort, to work around a potentially dangerous

A typical avalanche slope in the Colorado Rockies. (Photo by Ray Stebbins)

slope. This can be done by traveling along the top of ridges on one side or the other of the slide area.

Occasionally, however, you just can't find a way around a slope without crossing a potential slide area. While the mountaineer crosses such dangerous terrain constantly, the camper should do so only under extreme compulsion. For trying to outguess avalanches is a hazardous game.

If you must risk a dangerous slope, there are ways to minimize the danger. Make your crossing early in the morning, before the melt begins. Only one member of the party should cross at a time and he should be completely clear of danger before the next man starts. If you are carrying a pack, the straps should be loosened and the hip belt unfastened, as if you

This is a small slide area. Everyone can see and avoid the large, obvious avalanche slopes; therefore, it's the small, short ones that do most of the killing. (Photo courtesy of the U.S. Forest Service)

were preparing to cross a stream. And, for added safety, each man should have fifty to seventy-five feet of avalanche cord. (This is the parachute cord dyed a bright color that we mentioned in Chapter 1.) He ties one end of the cord to his belt and trails the rest out behind him as he crosses the slope. Then if he is swept away, the trailing cord may mark his location and speed up rescue.

If you start across an area and the snow makes a hollow sound, or any sound at all, retreat to safety at once. Den Davidson would say the snow is talking to you and it's saying, "Get the hell off!"

If you should get caught in a slide, treat it like water. Shrug off your pack, hold your breath, and swim like crazy. With luck you may be able to keep yourself close to the surface of the slide, and you might even be able to dig yourself out when it stops. At least your wild struggling may provide some breathing space as the snow sets up around you.

Chances of survival depend to a great extent on the density of the slide. Avalanches can range from powder dry, with as little as three percent moisture, to near solid slush with a sixty percent water content. Caught in a dry avalanche, the victim will smother immediately as the powdery snow fills his lungs. The wet snow on the other hand, will pack around the victim like cement, also smothering him in the process. Fortunately, most avalanches are in between these extremes. Often there is enough air in the snow to let the victim breathe for some time. At least one lucky hiker managed to survive for eight days packed in a snow slide because the sun melted along his ski pole forming a passage that brought him fresh air. He was found in excellent shape except for three frostbitten toes.

CORNICES

One usually thinks of cornices in connection with mountaineering. Yet you may encounter them if you are climbing a ridge to avoid a slide area. A cornice is merely a thin shelf of snow that has been carved from a sheer wall by the action of wind. The term, of course, means a decorative molding and, viewed from below, the graceful translucence of a cornice is a thing of beauty. From the top, it looks like solid snow, but if you step on it, the shelf breaks, plunging you into thin air. The obvious way to avoid the danger is to stay well back from any sheer snow wall.

High ridges are not the only places you will encounter cornices, for they have their low country equivalents. A friend of mine fell through a snow shelf just as we were returning from a trip. We were approaching the highway where we had left our car. The road had been plowed, leaving a sheer snow bank on each side that was twelve feet high. Wind and melt had undercut the wall and as my friend traveled along the edge, he

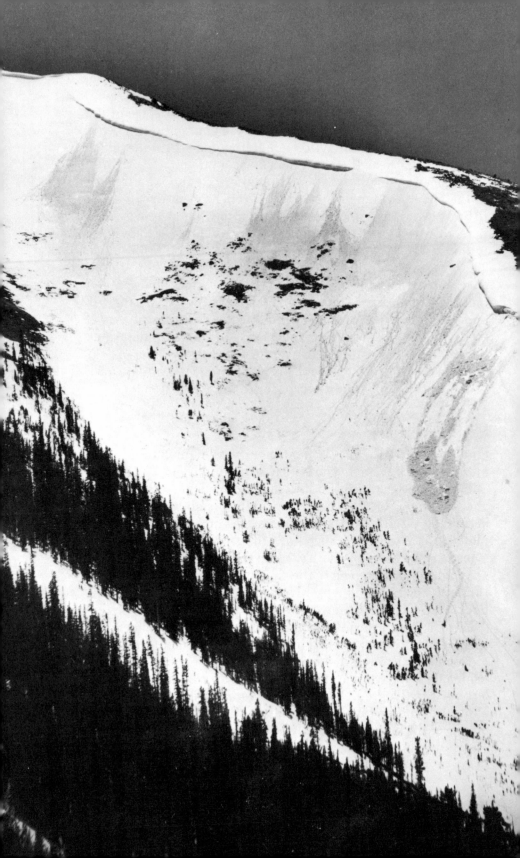

broke through the shelf. He suffered only a bad sprain and a broken snowshoe, but it could have been worse.

Since there isn't much you can do once you start falling through space, learn to be alert for any possible overhanging shelf, no matter where you are.

SNOW AND ICE BRIDGES

Snow and ice bridges are generally associated with glaciers, but the winter camper may find them any time he has to cross a small stream that has been covered with snow.

Bridges occur when the snow has formed an insulating layer over the stream and prevents the water from freezing. The action of the water and its comparative warmth will hollow out a tunnel along the stream bed. If the top of the tunnel is thin, the camper who tries to cross it will break through.

It's possible, though rare, to be badly hurt in such a fall, but even a bad sprain can be very serious in the back country, and cold weather makes it even more so. A greater problem arises, however, if the fall results in getting soaked. In sub-freezing temperatures, wet clothing can mean disaster.

For this reason, all experienced winter campers approach snow-covered streams with caution. It may be that with heavy snow cover, you won't realize that the stream is there. Just assume that even the smallest cut or ravine has a stream flowing through it. As you approach the center, probe with the handle end of your ski pole, or with your staff to make certain that the snow is solid.

Crossing larger streams and rivers also may prove hazardous. Running water or insulating snow can make for thin ice, while wind and erratic temperatures may produce the honeycomb effect typical of rotten ice. Such crossings can be made in relative safety if you proceed carefully, testing for weak spots at every step.

(Facing page) This large avalanche area has a well-defined cornice along the ridge line. (Photo courtesy of the U.S. Forest Service)

The existence of dangerous terrain should never discourage the camper from challenging the winter high country. These dangers can be avoided if the camper is constantly alert to possible problems. With a little caution and common sense, there is no reason why he cannot travel safely and freely through the high country. It is true that the beginner should first gain some experience in less difficult areas. And, since the high mountains in winter can be treacherous and unpredictable, all winter campers should be familiar with survival techniques and learn to carry a well-designed survival kit. (Both of these matters are discussed in Chapter 7.)

But with all precautions taken, I'd much rather travel rough country, smoothed by the snow, than to travel it in summer. Anyone who has ever worked across a scree slope or boulder-hopped for miles will fully appreciate the ease of traveling over deep snow. Besides, the pride and joy of conquering for your very own that rugged and indescribably beautiful country is well worth any effort.

DANGEROUS WEATHER — EXTREME COLD

The cold-weather camper doesn't have to be in the mountains or in deep snow to encounter trouble. Obviously, the cold itself presents danger. The various ways of keeping warm, discussed in the last chapter, are sufficient to avoid danger except under the most extreme conditions. Such conditions may arise, however, with a sudden, very steep drop in temperature. Certain signs will alert you to check your thermometer. For example, the day is clear and bright, but the sun seems to lack warmth. The snow underfoot doesn't crunch. It gives off a high pitched squeak, like a rubber heel being twisted on a polished floor. From time to time, the trees snap and pop explosively. Smoke from your fire stands straight in the air, seemingly motionless. The sharp edge of cold penetrates clothing that was adequate yesterday, and fingers stiffen the moment you remove your gloves. All of this indicates that the bottom has fallen out and that you are dealing with temperatures ranging down to -40 degrees F. or lower.

If you have camp set up, the simplest and safest thing to do is to stay there and warm yourself by the fire until the temperature moderates. As a camper, you should be under no compulsion to travel.

If, however, you are caught on the trail or forced to travel by an emergency, certain precautions should be observed. Deep breathing is out. Gulping down super-cooled air can frost the lungs. In severe conditions, it can cause freezing of lung tissue, with deadly results. So, keep the breathing slow and steady and don't get winded. This means moving at a careful and deliberate pace, so as not to create too great an oxygen demand. Physical activity helps keep you warm, but it shouldn't be overdone. Keep all flesh covered. This means you will want to use your face mask as well as goggles. And, now is the time to break out the chewing gum. The jaw action will stimulate blood flow to the ears and facial extremities.

From time to time, you should stop and check the ears and faces of the members of the group. Look for the telltale, shiny, dead white spots that might indicate frozen flesh. It may be necessary to stop and build a fire if anyone feels a numbness in hands or feet. Such lack of feeling could be an indication of frostbite.

Frostbite

Severe cold alone is seldom responsible for frostbite. Its occurrence depends very much on the physical condition of the camper. If he is tired, dehydrated, and hungry, as well as cold, he is an ideal prospect. So the easy way to avoid the problem is to stay warm and dry, avoid exhaustion, eat heartily and swill fluids.

Many outdoorsmen who spend much time in the cold have suffered from minor forms of frostbite. Permanent tissue damage usually was prevented by an instinctive reaction to warm the affected part. Yet the symptoms they felt were the same that lead to more severe forms, in which some permanent damage may occur.

In a case of frostbite, ice crystals are formed between the

cells of the tissue. If the affected part is not thawed, these crystals grow, drawing water from the cells. In a process not yet thoroughly understood, certain biochemical changes take place in the tissue. If these are not promptly reversed by warming, damage necessitating skin grafts and/or amputation will result. A critical point is reached when the affected area attains a temperature of five degrees below the freezing point of water. The process then becomes irreversible.

The first sign of developing frostbite is the feeling of sharply painful cold in the affected area. The pain becomes increasingly sharp, then fades as numbness sets in. If nothing is done, the area will actually begin to feel warm. This is a definite warning that the frostbite is progressing from a minor to a serious stage.

Over a minor frostbite the skin is waxy and yellowish to dead white and the flesh underneath is doughy, but still pliable. In severe cases, the skin may be reddish-blue in color, there usually is swelling and, in advanced stages, blisters; the flesh becomes hard and woody, which is nearly always a sign of frozen flesh and may mean some permanent damage.

Minor frostbite can be treated on the trail or in camp. Warm the affected part quickly and gently without any rubbing. Applying body heat usually is sufficient. Ears, cheeks, nose, and chin can be warmed by a cupped hand. Fingers can be placed in the armpits and the feet are probably best warmed against the abdomen of another member of the party or against your own leg, covered with your hands. Once a part is warmed, make certain that there is no refreezing. Thawing is usually followed by a tingling and burning sensation and a blotchy red appearance in the affected part. There may be some swelling. But remember, *do not rub the part at any time.*

Serious or deep frostbite occurs when the affected part is frozen hard. Do not try to treat such a condition in the field. Rather, make immediate plans to get the victim out to a doctor. Once a part is frozen, the damage is done and further exposure won't make it much more extensive. In fact, you can actually walk on frozen feet for days without doing them much further harm, whereas if you thawed them, the victim would have to be carried out.

Ideas regarding the treatment of frostbite have changed over the years. Recently new techniques have been developed and some old ideas debunked. Here are the latest rules for treating frostbite, whether minor or severe:

1)   Never try to rewarm a frozen part by exercising it. Such action increases the possibility of permanent tissue damage.

2)   Never rub a frozen part or area before, during, or after rewarming. Never rub a part with snow and never massage at any time.

3)   Never try to warm a frozen part by the heat of an open fire or stove. Severe burns could result. Even in cases of minor frostbite, you should warm your hand by the fire and place it over the affected part.

4)   Frozen flesh should be rapidly rewarmed in water held at between 108 and 112 degrees F. This procedure, however, should be handled only by a doctor or experienced first-aid man. It should not be attempted in the field or by the inexperienced.

Among campers, as opposed to mountaineers, the incidence of serious frostbite is rare. Even when it does occur, extensive tissue damage, requiring skin grafts or amputation, is likewise infrequent. Just remember that the risk of frostbite will remain minor so long as the camper gets his rest, eats well, stays warm and dry, and drinks plenty of fluids.

High Winds

We have already mentioned the dangers of high winds, or moderate winds and low temperatures. As a refresher, it is sufficient to recall the Army's "rule of thirty." A thirty-mile-an hour wind at -30 degrees F. will freeze exposed flesh in thirty seconds.

Freezing, however, is not the only danger presented by high

Wind is the winter camper's worst enemy. When it blows, snug down your tent and stay in camp. (Photo courtesy of Page Fagan)

Ski camper heads into a whiteout. (Photo by Ray Stebbins)

wind. It can also weaken and confuse a person. Even the healthiest and strongest camper is quickly reduced to a stumbling, uncoordinated hulk if he tries to travel against the wind. Weakened and disoriented, he is a prime prospect for trouble.

When caught by a wind, observe the simple safety rule well known to Eskimos, arctic wildlife, and experienced winter campers — get out of it. An Eskimo will stop at once and build an igloo. An animal will burrow into the snow, and the camper will pitch his tent. The idea is to get to shelter quickly and to stay there until the wind moderates.

Whiteout

Windblown or falling snow or fog or mist can create a condition known as a whiteout. In this case, the landscape loses all its features and contours, becoming a solid, smooth wall of white. It can happen with surprising suddenness when the landscape is covered with snow.

The camper caught in a whiteout quickly becomes disoriented and loses all sense of direction. Obviously, the danger is that he will become completely lost if he continues to travel. On occasion, some visibility will remain, and the camper who is traveling a well-known or well-marked trail, may proceed cautiously. But, he will want to have his compass in hand to keep himself continually oriented.

Whiteout also may occur on bright, sunny days in snow country when eyes become fatigued. Even though you are wearing dark glasses, your eyes blur and the features of the landscape seem to shift constantly. Usually this is not serious and merely stopping at intervals to rest your eyes will enable you to continue your trip.

OTHER TREACHEROUS CONDITIONS

The dangers of severe cold, high winds, or whiteout are obvious and easily understood. The signs are clear and precautions can be taken. There are other situations in which seemingly harmless weather conditions can become deadly — for the careless camper.

How many times have you picked up a newspaper to read that a hunter or camper became lost and was found dead a day or so later? The article usually reports that the victim died of exposure. If you check into the case, you may find that the temperatures were quite mild, perhaps as high as 40 or 50 degrees F. The wind during the period didn't exceed ten miles per hour, although there was precipitation in the form of rain or snow. Yet these seemingly mild conditions killed. In such cases, the victim allowed himself to get wet, fatigued, and dehydrated. Then, with a light wind working on him, he became another statistic.

Hypothermia

Death from exposure, whether in severe conditions or those as mild as described above, is caused by a process called hypothermia. It is simply a cooling of the body, including the area around the vital organs, to a point where vital functions break down. Every outdoorsman who ventures into the winter wilderness should thoroughly understand hypothermia. He should know how it occurs, its symptoms, and its treatment.

As pointed out previously, the body itself is the chief source of heat for the winter camper. We increase body heat by eating high calorie food to produce warmth directly and by using the energy it provides in the form of exercise, which also warms us. Our clothing, acting as an insulator, prevents the heat from dissipating too rapidly.

However, when a camper allows himself to be soaked by snow, rain, or even perspiration, his clothing will act as a conductor. Under the influence of the lightest breeze, wet clothing will drain heat from the body very rapidly. If the camper further reduces available heat by failing to eat and drink properly and by becoming so exhausted that exercise is decreased, his body may begin to lose more heat than it can replace. When this occurs, hypothermia has begun.

As body temperature drops a few degrees from 98.6 to 97 or 96 degrees F., the camper will begin to shiver, violently enough that such simple motor tasks as striking a match become difficult. If the heat loss continues, at about 92 to 91 degrees F. the shivering will come in spasms and at intervals. The victim will begin to have some trouble with his speech, and his motor coordination will continue to deteriorate. If he is hiking, he may begin to stumble. As his temperature drops to around 85 degrees F., his muscles will begin to stiffen and he may become somewhat irrational. At 80 degrees, as pulse and respiration slow, the victim will sink into a trance-like stupor. Below 80 degrees, he will become unconscious and, if the cooling is not arrested, death quickly follows.

In one case where the victim was soaked by immersion in water under severe arctic condtions, the entire process took place in slightly over three minutes. And even under relatively mild conditions, hikers on the trail have died from hypothermia in as little as thirty minutes. But in many instances, the loss of body heat occurs so slowly that the victim is not aware of it at all. It is this insidious nature of the process that makes hypothermia so dangerous.

Any time that weather conditions combine wind, cold, and wet, be on the alert for symptoms. If you, or any member of your party, begin to shiver uncontrollably, stop and set up a shelter at once, for you must get the victim out of the wind immediately. Strip off all of his wet clothing and replace it with dry things. If no extra clothing is available, have other members of the group take off some of theirs to give the victim. Feed him hot food and drink as well as high energy foods.

To help the warming process, build fires on two sides of the shelter. If the shivering continues, get the victim into a sleeping bag that has been warmed by another member of the party. It may be necessary to double the bags and use the warm bodies of the others to warm the victim. In serious cases, it may take six to eight hours of care. When the victim is finally rewarmed, be very careful not to let him chill, and get him out to a doctor as soon as possible.

Though hypothermia is extremely dangerous, prevention is quite simple. On windy days, take extra care to stay dry, both inside and out. Be aware that in winter, chilling is always dangerous. Eat well and drink plenty of fluids and don't allow yourself to become exhausted. Never hesitate to stop and put on wet gear, build a fire, or set up camp if at any time you feel the symptoms of chilling.

Most victims of hypothermia are those who become lost and separated from both their companions and their equipment. Under these circumstances, it is often difficult to stay dry and to feed yourself properly. But the camper who keeps his wits and his confidence is the one who survives. It is the inexperienced, the careless, and above all, the panic-stricken who perishes.

Panic

In the fall of 1974, a forty-eight-year-old elk hunter was lost in Montana's Garnet Range. His hunting companions had dropped him off in early morning in an area he had never hunted. The temperature at the time was only 20 degrees F., but there was wind and snow. The effective temperature was probably around zero. Yet it was not a dangerous situation for an experienced and warmly dressed hunter.

That evening, however, he failed to return to the pickup point and the next morning his friends reported him missing. A search was organized at once and his body was found that afternoon. Apparently he had died sometime in the morning. His tracks, wandering in circles, indicated that he was completely lost. The length between strides showed that at times he had been running, which clearly suggested wild panic. As further indication of his desperate state of mind, it was determined that he had hiked all night, never stopping to build a fire. Nor did he make an attempt to set up a camp. He died, of course, of hypothermia, but he was killed by his own panic.

Such panic is nearly always the result of that sudden, gut-grabbing fear that strikes when the camper says to himself,

"Oh-my-God-I'm-really-lost!" Even the most experienced outdoorsman usually suffers some bad moments before he regains his composure.

In such a situation, you are advised, by every survival manual ever written, not to panic. Good advice, but it can be tough to follow. The fact is, you'll be an unusual specimen if you don't get a bit spooky when you realize you are lost in a winter wilderness.

To avoid critical mistakes, prepare yourself ahead of time. Be aware that you might get lost and coach yourself to take a few very important steps. The first is, STOP. Then, taking your time, find or make a comfortable place to SIT. This is important because it is impossible to think productively while you are moving through the woods; action and thought don't mix. So, only after you are solidly settled are you ready for the next important step, THINK.

You can start by reminding yourself that the odds are all in your favor. Of the hundreds of campers, hunters, skiers, and snowmobilers who get lost each year, all but a few find their own way out. Another small group has to be found and only a very tiny portion fail to survive. The latter usually get into trouble because they failed to do what you have already done; they failed to stay calm.

In fact, by now you may be so calm you will remember that traveling in snow will leave a back trail that even Aunt Minnie could follow. All you have to do is trace your own tracks back to recognizable country, or all the way out, if necessary. Even with no snow, you may be able to think back calmly and to figure out just where you went wrong.

Being Lost

If, however, there seems to be no way out at the moment, then it's time for the next step, PLAN. Perhaps there are friends in the area who will be looking for you. Wait! Don't leap up and start fire making, shouting, or banging on trees. Get all of your planning done before you make that first move.

The major decision you will face is whether to stay in one spot and wait to be found or to try and find your own way out. If there are no others on the trip to start looking for you, it's still possible to estimate about when a search would begin. Statistics show that individuals are reported lost from ten to twenty-four hours after they fail to return as planned. This, of course, may have some bearing on your choice.

About now, you will be feeling another kind of pressure — that of dread and embarrassment as you envision the sheriff's posse and half a hundred hearty volunteers mustering to find the "clown who got lost." Don't let this affect your decision. Just remember that the searchers are getting a rare chance to exercise their skills, of which they are undoubtedly very proud. Further, you are probably providing them the only excitement they may have for the entire, otherwise drab winter. Instead, base your choice of whether to go or stay put on the facts of your particular situation.

Carefully assess just how good the chances are of getting out on your own. Perhaps you can remember the general direction of your travel. Were you heading into the sun most of the time? Or maybe there is some major locator such as a river, a highway, or large valley that you could strike by traveling in a certain direction. That is, do you know this locator has to lie, say south of your present location and that it is long enough east and west so that you couldn't miss it if you traveled generally south? Possibly you remember cutting some well used and well marked path or snowmobile trail. Could you find it again? (Beware of false friends; old trails and logging roads can lead you away from help as well as toward it.) Is there a high point you could climb to and get yourself oriented? Are there farms or ranches in the area you might find? Could you follow a stream out? A fence line? Do you personally know of any outstanding landmarks in the area that you could recognize, such as a mountain peak, a lake, or a large valley? Is the area settled enough so that walking a given number of miles in any direction will take you to civilization?

These are the questions you will have to ask in order to make your decision. If you answer yes to one or more of the above and other factors seem to be on your side, then you may want to try and find your way out. On the other hand, you may have no specific clues as to where you are. Or, there may be friends in the area who will begin searching. The weather may be vicious or perhaps you are injured. Maybe you have no compass and have forgotten how to find north. Or, maybe out of sheer laziness, you may decide to stay put.

In fact, staying in one place offers some distinct advantages. You won't have to set up or build a new camp every night. You will have the time and energy to set up signal fires. There will be no danger of walking out of the possible search area. By staying put, you can more surely avoid the dangers of hypothermia and it is the best way to conserve both food and energy. It's possible to stay hidden from searchers for a long time, even in a relatively small area, if you keep moving. In short, if searchers are likely to be involved, your chances are better if you stay in one spot.

FIRST AID

Though the panic which results from being lost is one of the most common causes of injuries, they also can happen through carelessness or sheer bad luck. Even minor injuries can be serious when they occur in the winter wilderness. Therefore, everyone who plans to do much winter camping should know basic first aid. Being able to treat injuries calmly and efficiently in a way that minimizes the chance of permanent damage is very important — and may make a life-or-death difference in some situations.

Whatever plans you make and whatever difficulties you encounter, your chances for success will be greatly increased if you remain calm. If at any time you become doubtful about the situation, remember to STOP, SIT, THINK, and PLAN.

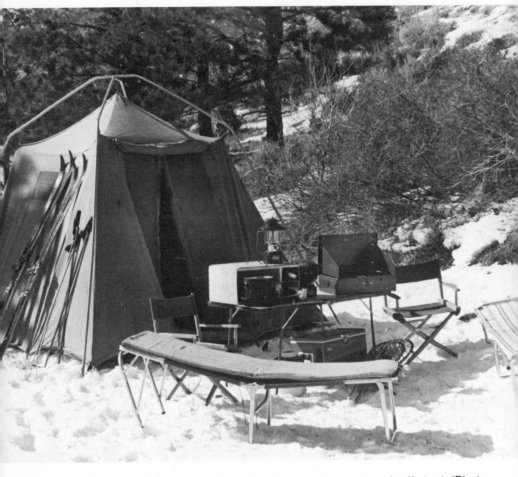

This tent camper's gear is ready to be moved into an umbrella tent. (Photo by Ray Stebbins)

6

How to Use a Base Camp

Not everyone who enjoys cold-weather camping is able or willing to carry his home on his back. For those who aren't, the greater comfort and convenience of a base camp is more appealing.

A base camp can be any type of shelter that is set up or parked in a given area and from which the camper can make day trips into the winter wilderness. Today, there is an incredible choice available, ranging from a simple family tent, with or without wheels, to a luxurious travel trailer or motor home. And an increasing number of camp grounds, both public and private, are beginning to cater to the cold-weather camper. From them, he can hike, ski tour, snowshoe, or snowmobile all day and return at evening to his comfortable base camp.

TENTS

For many of us who did our first camping under canvas,

nothing will ever quite replace the family tent. There is something about the scent of warm canvas that will always suggest the freedom and excitement of the outdoors. And the tent still offers some advantages worth considering.

As a winter base camp, it is itself a luxury compared to the tiny backpacker's tent. It is roomier, homier, warmer, and free from problems of frost. Its initial cost is relatively low, and a good quality tent will give years of service. It is ideal for family use, especially for young couples on a tight budget. Moreover, if you already have a roomy, stable tent with good head space, it may very well do for winter as well as summer camping. And, since most of the equipment you use with it can also be used in cold weather, tent camping may be the easiest and least expensive way for you to make the winter scene.

If you don't have a tent but plan to buy one with cold-weather camping in mind, the variety of models available may be somewhat confusing. However, designs suitable for winter can be narrowed down quickly to a few standard types.

We can eliminate at once the old classic, open-face jobs such as the baker and the Whelen, as well as all versions of the tepee, no matter how modern. Their use is too specialized. And the old wall tent, still a favorite with some big game hunters, is not suitable for leisure camping because of its complexity, bulk, and lack of flooring. The expedition or explorer design, with its tepee-like roof, doesn't have sufficent head room. Though handy and very stable, the new pop-up types don't generally come in sizes large enough for winter use. This narrows the choice to only a few designs.

Types of Tents

Umbrella Tent. Perhaps the most popular and practical tent for winter camping is the umbrella tent. Originally made with a center pole and interior metal ribs that opened like an umbrella, the modern version has a light aluminum, exterior frame from which the tent hangs. This not only provides more space inside, but greatly increases stability.

This 10- by 10-foot umbrella tent is very stable and is easy to set up. It will provide a comfortable winter shelter for two campers. (Photo by Ray Stebbins)

The base of the tent is square and usually consists of heavy, waterproof canvas. The walls slope in slightly to a square top with a center peak, so there is excellent head room. On one side is a large door opening, covered by canvas flaps and bugproof netting that zips closed. On the better tents, there also is an exterior storm flap that doubles as a large awning. Floor sizes range from a small seven-by-seven feet to the large twelve-by-twelve and the center height from seven to ten feet.

The simple and practical design of the umbrella tent is particularly well adapted to winter use. It can be easily set up by one man in ten minutes. More important for cold-weather camping, however, is its excellent stability in wind.

The capacity of all tents is more limited in winter camping. Since you'll do most of your cooking and living inside in cold weather, you'll need plenty of space. In addition to bunks, you'll want room for personal gear, a table, and some small folding chairs. This means that generally a ten-by-ten umbrella is about right for two campers. The twelve-by-twelve can handle four, but three is much better. You can crowd in more people by carefully stowing gear and bunks during the day and then putting away the tables and chairs at night. You'll find, however, that such close living, though acceptable in summer, is much too close in winter.

One solution for campers who need more space is a modified version of the umbrella tent. In this model, a side room or extension is built onto the basic tent. This increases capacity with only minor effect on stability. Dimensions will vary, but the average ten-foot umbrella with an extension will give you a ten-by-sixteen floor size. This tent is large enough to provide deluxe living for four campers or uncrowded living for five.

Some models are available with two such extensions, offering a floor area of ten-by-twenty-two feet. This size, however, is bulky, heavy, and awkward to handle. If you need this much space, you might be better off with two smaller tents.

Cabin Tent. Another design suitable for comfortable winter camping is the cabin or cottage tent. The floor is rectangular and the straight side walls rise to a cabin-type roof. These tents are also provided with exterior aluminum frames. Popular sizes range from eight-by-ten feet to the large ten-by-sixteen. This design requires slightly heavier tent cloth, which generally means higher cost. Its main drawback for winter camping, however, is the fact that it is somewhat less stable than the umbrella tent. Nevertheless, it is a roomy, comfortable design that makes a good choice in areas where high wind is no problem.

Choosing a Tent

In order to select a tent, it helps to know something about the materials used in their construction. The term canvas is

One of Coleman's versions of the cottage or cabin tent. (Photo courtesy of the Coleman Company)

misleading, for it is often used to refer to any of the cotton cloths used in tent making. Probably the term should be confined to cotton duck. This is a heavy, single weave material used in most wall tents and in some army applications. For general use, however, it is too stiff and bulky.

Most leisure tents are made of a tight-weave cotton drill and, less often, a heavy poplin. Weight of the cloth is important and is usually given in the supplier's description of the tent. It is quoted in ounces per square yard. Though weights given for the same material may vary slightly since some manufacturers weigh their material after treatment for waterproofing. Most cotton tent cloths will run from six ounces to about eight and a half ounces.

Recently, some tent makers have come out with nylon

versions of the standard tent designs. It makes a much lighter
tent, of course, but when you consider that the average ten-by-
ten umbrella tent, complete with pegs, poles, and rope, won't
run more than forty pounds, the lightness of nylon isn't much
of an advantage. Nylon has to be heavily coated to really turn
water, in which case it sweats badly. If it isn't coated, you'll
have to cover it with an extra fly, just as you would an
uncoated mountain tent. Less suitable than cotton for large
tents, nylon also is more expensive. If that isn't deterrent
enough, consider how impossible it would be to develop any
nostalgia for a tent that smells like chemicals instead of
canvas.

If I were in the market today for a winter tent for two
campers, I'd probably go with the ten-by-ten umbrella or an
eight-by-twelve cabin style. These figures, by the way, are
outside dimensions. In either tent, the height at the eaves
should be close to six feet and in no case less than five and a
half. Nylon is the best material for the netting on doors and
windows. I'd require an exterior aluminum frame, preferably
with friction-tightening poles. There are a few umbrella tents
around with only two support poles that hold a square upper
frame. I'd stay away from that design since it won't stand
much wind. For flooring, I prefer a heavy waterproof canvas
that extends up the wall four or five inches. This is a particularly good feature for winter since it protects against seepage
from melting snow that lies along the bottom edge of the tent.

At this writing, you can buy a good ten-by-ten umbrella tent
for about $120, complete with rope, pegs, and poles. For the
cabin model in a comparable size, I'd figure on $160 and about
the same for an umbrella with extension.

Today, if I were in the market for a tent, I'd take a close look
at Herter's ten-by-ten umbrella. It's made of eight-ounce drill
and the wall height is six foot three inches, which should
provide plenty of head room. It sells for about $112.

There is also an interesting model put out by Thermos
Company, called the Prairie Schooner. It looks like one, or like
the top of a sheep wagon, but this design should take a lot of

wind. The curved roof is supported by fiberglass poles and, with a center height of six feet two inches, it should offer fair head room. The material here is eight-ounce drill. The tent comes in two sizes, both are six feet six inches wide and the lengths are nine and twelve feet respectively. I'd only be interested in the larger one. Though it doesn't sound like much floor space, two campers could put their bunks crosswise in the back and have almost thirty square feet of living space in the front. This one sells for about $158.

In any case, I'd do some shopping and comparing. A tent that is suited to your particular needs can be both a pleasure and a good investment. It's worth spending some time and effort on its purchase.

TENTING ACCESSORIES

Bedding

For really comfortable tent camping, a bunk is a must. It raises you off the floor and out of the drafts. And being just a few feet off the ground when you sleep will put you in warmer air. In addition to providing a place to sit during the day, a cot is one of the amenities that adds a touch of civilization to the wilderness.

There are several types of tent cots available. The old, wooden-framed, canvas-covered army cot is still around. It's a bit awkward and not too comfortable but is very inexpensive. Much better are those that have aluminum frames covered with canvas or nylon. They fold in the middle and the legs lie flat for storage or travel. Most have continuous U-shaped legs rather than straight legs, which can wear holes in the tent floor. A ratchet setting on some models allows them to be used as lounge chairs as well as beds. Others have convenient options that permit you to use them singly or as double- or even triple-decker bunks. This feature is a great space saver and ideal for campers with children. The canvas types are cheaper than the nylon, but only by a matter of a few dollars.

Both of these bunks have aluminum frames, but one employs springs and the other solid nylon to support the mattress. (Photo by Ray Stebbins)

Another type of cot uses link springs instead of a cover and, of course, includes a mattress pad. It makes for a softer bed if that's what you want. If the mattress is made of cotton, then it's a good idea to use your foam or Ensolite pad on top. Cotton can absorb moisture, and the pad will keep it away from your sleeping bag.

Whatever combination of bedding you use, I wouldn't advise an air mattress. They date back to the dark ages of camping and make a cold, hard bed — on those occasions when they do stay inflated.

A sleeping bag will complete your bedding. Chances are you already have one for summer use. Since you'll have a tent heater to keep things warm at night, the summer bag may be heavy enough for winter tenting. In Chapter 1, we discussed the types of bags and the warmth they deliver. Reading this should give you an idea of what your bag will do. Roughly, if it will handle zero degree temperature, it should be all right.

If you decide that your summer bag is too light, it can still be used as a liner. For very little money, you can get a good quality bag with three pounds of Dacron 88 fill. Almost any summer bag inside the Dacron job would do for tenting, and the new bag can be used alone in summer.

Since bulk and weight aren't much of a problem to the tent camper, Dacron also is the least expensive route if you are buying a bag just for cold-weather tenting. In this case, you'll need one with five pounds of fill. A good one will run about $40-$45, but the equivalent warmth in down would cost over $100.

For my winter tenting, I use a light bag with one pound of prime goose down fill inside another with two pounds of fill. I use this combination because I happen to prefer down. All considerations of warmth and price aside, nothing beats the sheer comfort of goose feathers for cold-weather sleeping.

Heaters, Stoves, Lanterns

These items are essential for a comfortable winter tent. They are grouped together since they all use one of two types of fuels, either white gasoline or propane. There isn't too much difference in the initial cost of either type gear, though some propane equipment is slightly higher. The main difference is in the ease and cost of operation. Equipment using gasoline is slightly more complex to use, but its fuel is less expensive by about a third. The propane gear is as simple to use as turning a dial and lighting a match. I've used both and had very little trouble with either one.

Tent Heaters. In catalytic tent heaters, propane definitely has the edge. Those burning white gas have to be primed outside the tent by covering the top of the element with gasoline and setting it afire. If not done properly, the catalyst won't start. Even then it takes twenty minutes or so for the heat to develop. The propane models, on the other hand, light with a match and begin producing heat in less than a minute.

My own preference in a tent heater is the Primus model 2513. It angles the heat in two directions and is adjustable from 2,000 to 8,000 BTUs. This size heater is adequate for tents

Interior setup of tent camper. Note the tent heater and the insulated jug and ice chest, which become, for the winter camper, a means of keeping food and water from freezing. (Photo by Ray Stebbins)

up to ten-by-twelve feet. For larger tents, there is model 2320 which will put out 10,000 BTUs. Since these heaters are offered by various suppliers, it's a good idea to do some price comparing. I've seen the identical model advertised by two different suppliers at prices $20 apart.

Whatever you buy, make certain it has an adjustment feature. There are nights in winter when 2,000 BTUs are more than enough and others when 8,000 will barely keep the eggs from freezing.

Stoves. When it comes to stoves, it's more of a tossup. I've used the same Coleman gasoline stove for fifteen years. It has never given me any trouble, nor have I ever replaced a part. Since my equipment sees more hard service than that of the average camper, this kind of reliability is impressive. On the other hand, many campers prefer the propane stove. Not only is it easier to operate, but the burners have a much finer adjustment and the new models are much easier to keep clean.

If I were buying a stove of either type, I'd get the three-burner style, despite the extra cost. Three burners will handle all meals more quickly and efficiently.

Lanterns. As for lanterns, I'd have to give the edge to the gasoline models, despite the stench they leave in the tent when you turn them off. They are very reliable and economical to operate. Moreover, I've had problems with the propane lanterns that use the small, throw-away cans of fuel. These small cans are provided with a rubber nipple which acts as a seal. The seal is opened by pushing the can onto the stem of a needle valve on the bottom of the lantern. On several of the lanterns I've used, slow leakage wasted fuel. The small orifice on the lanterns also plugged up. It doesn't happen all at once, but the light gets dimmer and dimmer, until you have to tear it down and clean it out. When, that is, you can find the tiny wire that is provided for the purpose.

Fuel. You should know as much as possible about the storage and heating properties of your fuel.

If you already own or plan to buy propane equipment, I'd strongly recommend using the large, refillable propane bottle, rather than any of the throw-away types. It's more economical and convenient, and you are less likely to run out of fuel. In addition, you can rig the bottle to operate as many as three different appliances. Primus has a thirteen-pound bottle that will hold eleven pounds of liquid propane. By simply weighing the bottle, you can always tell how much fuel you have left. A full bottle will provide about 230,000 BTUs. By dividing the BTU rated output of your appliance into the total BTUs available, you can determine how long it will operate. For example, if your tent heater is set at 5,000 BTUs, dividing 5,000 into 230,000, you'll find you can count on forty-six hours of continuous operation. With the small, throw-away bottles, it's difficult to keep track, and there is always the possibility you'll leave the extras at home.

Most of the gasoline-burning equipment requires white gas

or a special fuel sold by the manufacturer. The latter is more expensive, but is cleaner burning and has less odor. It can be purchased at most sporting goods dealers, while the white gas is sometimes hard to find. It is usually sold at filling stations that cater to sportsmen. If you use white gas, be sure your container is clean and use a filter funnel to fill the fuel tank. Unleaded gasoline should not be used in equipment that burns white gas except in emergencies. Regular use will cause problems due to the additives used in the gasoline.

In some areas of the country you will find bottles of butane sold for camping fuel. Don't use these for winter camping. LPG fuels (liquid petroleum gas) must vaporize in order to burn. Propane will vaporize at temperatures down to -44 degrees F., but butane will not vaporize at temperatures below 32 degrees F. Obviously, butane is not a winter fuel.

If you haven't already purchased the equipment, one of the best ways to decide between propane and gasoline is to rent or borrow the gear and try it. In any case, as long as you buy the equipment from a reliable manufacturer, either type will give you years of good service.

Other Equipment

With a few other miscellaneous items, winter tenting can be a nearly luxurious experience.

If you have already done plenty of summer camping, you've no doubt discovered that a folding table and a small camp chair for each camper is a great convenience. These are inexpensive items that are even more necessary for the indoor living of cold-weather camping.

Most summer campers already have a thunder box. For those unfamiliar with the term, it is a wooden box with shelves and a small drawer or two. Usually it is fitted with a drop lid that serves as a counter area. It holds pots, pans, dishes, eating utensils, and condiments. Not only does it make for a neater, more convenient camp kitchen, but it saves time when you are loading gear for a trip. At home, it can be kept cleaned and ready, and all you have to do is throw the box in the vehicle

Tent camper's gear includes thunder box, gasoline lantern, stove, and folding table. (Photo by Ray Stebbins)

when you leave on a trip. There is no need to hunt up kitchen gear and no worry about leaving some essential cooking equipment at home.

For cold-weather camping, you will need extra insulated jugs for water. The jugs will keep the water from freezing if you shut off your tent heater during the day while you are gone. If temperatures are severe, it is a good idea to add a pan of hot water to each jug before you leave for the day.

For the same reason, certain foods with a high water content such as eggs, milk, and soft drinks should be kept in an insulated cooler, which for the winter camper becomes a warm box. It helps to add a hand warmer to the cooler if temperatures are very low.

Campers generally develop huge appetites at any time of the year, and this is particularly true of winter campers. And, as we have already pointed out, plenty of high calorie food is needed to keep you warm. This makes cold-weather camping a joy for those of us who can gain weight by merely taking a deep breath. In a winter camp, you can and, in fact, should eat plenty of foods that are high in fats and carbohydrates. A day of snowshoeing, ski touring, or snowmobiling will take care of the calories. You may not lose weight by strenuous winter activities, but it will certainly get distributed better.

Freeze-dried foods, though handy, are an unnecessary expense for the tent camper. He can enjoy fresh foods and canned goods without concern over bulk and weight. It helps to bring some one-dish dinners prepared at home. Chili, stews, and pasta dishes all go well in cold weather. Having them ready ahead saves time, effort, and fuel in camp. As an added advantage of cold weather, you can take perishable foods that wouldn't keep well in summer, for your ice box is the whole outdoors.

In addition to clothing, food, and equipment, you may want to include some books, cards, and perhaps some box games, if there are children in the group. These will come in handy if a stormy day keeps you in the tent.

You will want to make a good check list, just as the backpacker does. It is your best insurance against leaving something essential at home. To develop a list, go through in your mind everything you will do on the trip. Think of setting up the tent, your bedding, the camp kitchen, and so forth. As you think through these actions, write down the equipment you need for each one. Once you have your list, use it. Don't check off an item until it is actually loaded in the vehicle.

If there is no snow on the ground when you reach your camping area, there shouldn't be much problem in setting up your tent. If there is snow and it isn't deep, you can clear it away. Deep snow should be stomped down as solidly as possible. Once an area the size of the tent has been tamped down to prevent the development of lumpy floors, it should be covered with a three-mil plastic sheet and your tent pitched on top. The plastic sheet will keep the tent floor from icing up and insulate against the cold. You may have to use rocks or logs to tie down the tent if the ground is frozen solid.

For a finishing touch, use some old scraps of carpet for a throw rug in front of your bunk. One friend of mine always takes a full nine-by-nine carpet to line the floor of his tent. It's a hassle to carry, but it sure makes for a warm, cozy shelter.

Tenting in winter isn't all that different and the transition for the summer camper should be easy. Once you've made the move and experience your favorite campground in all its winter beauty, you'll be glad you did.

RVs AS BASE CAMPS

RVs (recreational vehicles) include tent trailers, camper trailers, pickup campers, travel trailers, and motor homes. As a result of the growing popularity of winter activities, more campers are taking to the ski slopes, snowmobile trails, and campground in RVs. Responding to this increased demand, more manufacturers are winterizing their equipment for cold-weather use. Even so, the majority of RVs are not built to withstand the extremes of winter cold.

The major problems involved in the cold-weather use of RVs are freeze-up of water systems, holding tanks, and drain lines. Maintaining the output of batteries is a challenge, too. However, by not using sinks and toilets, by draining all tanks and lines, and by using gasoline or propane lanterns for light, RV owners avoid the hassles and still have soft beds, the warmth of a propane furnace, a kitchen-type range for cooking, plenty of storage space, and generally more comfortable quarters. In short, an excellent base camp is provided by their unwinterized RV.

As to which kinds of RVs are most suitable for cold-weather camping, each has both advantages and drawbacks.

Tent Trailers and Camper Trailers

Tent trailers and camper trailers are two terms that describe the same basic type of RV. The difference is in the amount and kind of special equipment provided. A tent trailer is just that, a

Camper trailers are fine for summer but do not make good winter base camps. (Photo courtesy of the Thetford Corporation)

tent on wheels. It is raised manually out of a low, compact trailer, which may be as large as seven-by-fourteen or as small as four-by-seven feet. The trailer itself forms the floor and part of the walls of the tent. The top, split in the middle, folds out to form two bunks on each end. A folding, hinged frame supports the canvas top. In the basic models, you use the same heating, cooking, and lighting gear that you would use in a regular tent. There are fancier types that offer a built-in folding table, propane equipment, and a battery for interior lighting. Since they offer very little advantage over a good tent, yet cost four to six times more, I couldn't recommend them for use any time of year.

Camper trailers are another matter. Though they also provide a tent on wheels, it's generally one with a hard top and many deluxe features. Though they also fold down into a low, compact profile, they offer a complete propane system with furnace and range-type stove, and have water and electrical systems and the option of hooking up to campground facilities. Some of the plush models even include bathrooms and holding tanks. In short, they offer a super tent with many of the same comforts found in the average travel trailer. And, they cost almost as much.

Camper trailers have some advantages over other RVs and some decided disadvantages as well. Their lower profile and lighter weight make them easier to tow and enable them to be pulled by a smaller, less powerful car. Their compact size also permits parking in a limited space. Their greatest advantage in winter is that they are easier to handle in wind and on icy roads.

On the other hand, with most models, the tent must be raised to reach food or equipment stored inside, which can be a considerable inconvenience. And, since most have a power system to raise the tent, you may have problems with the mechanism in very cold weather.

Their greatest disadvantage, however, is that they are impossible to insulate. Consequently, in severe cold, it is difficult to keep the camper warm enough to insure proper operation of equipment. Thus, you may end up with a some-what more comfortable tent on wheels.

Pickup Campers

A pickup camper is, essentially, a cabin that slides onto the bed of a pickup or is bolted directly onto the truck chassis. Models range from bare wall simplicity to deluxe, self-contained jobs that can be used in primitive areas where no hook-ups are available. Such an RV must have cooking, heating, and lighting facilities, as well as a water system. It also will have a toilet and either a shower or tub. Since there is no room for a holding tank, the toilet generally is a portable type, which actually is an advantage in cold weather, for there is no need to worry about the freeze-up of holding tank and drain lines. Of the two kinds, the self-contained models make the most comfortable base camps.

These campers are easy to insulate, and a winterized job can handle most any cold-weather situation. The fancier models can use the hook-up facilities of the winterized campgrounds. And pickup campers are a favorite of the snowmobilers, since it's easy to tow a trailer load of snowmachines behind the truck.

On the other hand, they are quite heavy and require at least a three-quarter-ton truck to carry them. The large campers are expensive, too. If you don't already own a suitable pickup, the purchase of a truck and camper can represent a large invest-ment. Moreover, interior space is limited by the necessarily narrow walk-through area.

Large campers will never win a prize for road handling. Since they weigh a good deal and sit high in the truck, the load is always top-heavy and the square, bulky shape offers plenty of wind resistance. Also, design requirements place the water tank on one side and, when full, its weight is hard to counter-balance. All of this makes for an awkward driving load, which can be a problem in high winds and on slick roads. So while most camper owners would argue that their rigs are easier to handle than a towed RV, they probably don't offer that much advantage in winter driving.

But they do offer comfort and few problems with freeze-up, so pickup campers are an excellent choice for a winter base camp.

Travel Trailers and Fifth Wheelers

Travel trailers range from a tiny fourteen-foot model to a huge thirty-foot home (usually measured from the hitch to the rear bumper or outside rear wall). The most popular sizes, however, are those between eighteen and twenty-two feet. Most of the popular models are self-contained, offering sleeping facilities for four to six people, comfortable dinette areas, complete kitchens, and a separate bathroom. In relation to the amenities they provide, they are the least expensive of the RVs.

The fifth wheeler offers, in addition, a bedroom alcove in the forward part of the trailer that extends out over the tow vehicle, usually a pickup. The hitch is located on the underside of the alcove and is the same type as that used by commercial trailer trucks. This arrangement makes for a roomier trailer that is remarkably easy to tow. It is also considerably more expensive than the standard type of trailer.

Considered as a group, the self-contained trailers are by far the roomiest and most comfortable of all RVs. As a base camp, they offer the advantage of home-like facilities and are especially suitable for the camper who takes his rig to a winterized campground for a relatively long stay.

Most manufacturers do not winterize their trailers, and not all of those who do prepare them to withstand severe temperatures. Since the water tank and water lines are contained in the upper, insulated portion of the trailer, they usually present no problem as long as the RV is well heated. The difficulty lies with the holding tank and drain lines. These are located on the underside of the trailer and are generally exposed to the wind and cold.

To properly winterize a trailer, the manufacturer covers the lines and the holding tank with heavy insulation. Then, the entire underside of the trailer is enclosed with an insulated shell. Even then it is a good idea to use an approved, non-alcohol based antifreeze in the holding tank and in the P-traps of all drain lines.

Since road conditions can be far from ideal in winter, many campers consider a towed vehicle unsuitable for winter use. However, you can learn to handle your trailer on ice and snow. You'll want an equalizing hitch that includes a sway control. It's expensive, but the first time you hit a slick spot on a dry road, you'll agree that it has paid for itself. On snow or ice, always drive slowly and don't use your engine drag to slow down as this may cause the rear wheels of your tow vehicle to skid. If you do skid, use the separate control to apply the *trailer brakes only*. This will straighten out and align the tow vehicle and trailer.

In deep snow, let the momentum carry you through with only a minimum application of power. If you should get stuck, be sure to have both vehicle and trailer towed out together without unhitching. Chains should be used on the tow vehicle, but neither snow tires nor chains are needed on the trailer.

Taking a trailer out in winter requires some planning, since the spot where you plan to set up may be deep in snow. You'll want to know that at the end of your drive, there will be a place to park. So, it's a good idea to check with your state travel bureau or with someone in the area where you plan to camp.

Motor Homes and Mini Homes

These RVs range from camper-like accommodations on a one ton chassis and camper vans with pop-up roofs to super luxurious homes on wheels. Since prices presently run from $9,000 for a simple van to more than $30,000 for the deluxe motor homes, the obvious drawback is cost. They are, however, the most maneuverable and the easiest to drive of all RVs, which makes them a good choice for winter roads. The

Winnebago's motor homes can provide deluxe winter base camps. (Photo courtesy of Winnebago Industries)

problems of winterizing are about the same as that of the travel trailer, though the more expensive models are usually well insulated and therefore more easily adaptable to winter use. Like the pickup camper, they appeal to snowmobilers because they can tow a small trailer. Though not as roomy as the average trailer, the larger motor homes can make an excellent base camp.

Winter Use of RVs

Most manufacturers of RVs designed for winter use encourage

the owners to become thoroughly familiar with their equipment and its operating capabilities in warm weather before attempting cold-weather use. They also have some good advice for those who use their equipment in winter.

Cobra Industries produces a line of RVs that are well insulated and specifically designed for cold-weather camping, and they offer suggestions in their owner's manual. They point out that there must *always* be heat in the RV during winter use. This means your furnace will be operating twenty-four hours a day. For this reason, two fuel bottles should be used and they should be closely watched. When one is emptied, it should be refilled as soon as possible. To help retain heat in the RV, keep the curtains closed and cover the air conditioner with one of the commercially available caps. At least one window should be slightly open, however, to allow moist air to escape and prevent excessive condensation.

The gas range or oven should *never* be used for additional heating. All other gas appliances in RVs are vented to the outside and can be used continuously. Cooking appliances, however, are not vented and should be used only for preparing meals. Also, when they are in use, make sure a vent or window is open to replenish the air supply.

If you are not connected to outside electricity, keep the use of lights and electrical appliances to a minimum. Power in the auxiliary battery generally won't last more than a day in sub-zero temperatures. If your RV is equipped with a battery charger, running the vehicle's engine at a fast idle for an hour should bring your battery back to about half-charge. Of course, before leaving home, you'll want to make certain that your electrical system is in top shape.

If you have a hot water heater, keep the pilot on at all times to guard against freeze-up. To insure proper draining and as additional protection, add antifreeze to holding tanks and the P-traps of all drain lines. Be certain to use only antifreeze approved for use with ABS plastic plumbing. *Never use automotive or alcohol-based antifreeze in your RV plumbing.*

With these suggestions and with a little planning ahead, anyone should be able to enjoy his RV as a winter base camp. After all, any RV represents a large amount of cash tied up in equipment, which can only be justified by the amount of use and pleasure you derive from it. By extending your camping season into winter, you are not only enjoying more of the outdoors, but you are getting a much better return on your recreational investment.

7

What to See and Do

An acquaintance of mine who had never done any cold-weather camping once asked me what anyone could possibly find to do in a winter wilderness.

"Don't you get bored?" he demanded.

The question startled me; then I realized that for the uninitiated, it was a natural thing to ask. And the answer is simple: No. There is too much to do, far more than you can ever get done.

The backpacker, of course, spends a good deal of his time just getting there, setting up camp, and handling the usual camp chores. For many packers, this is enough. To conquer the winter wilderness and enjoy its very special quality is sufficient activity and reward in itself. Others, while they enjoy the camping, go into the back country for some purpose. They want to snowshoe, ski, ride snowmobiles, photograph, fish, or maybe polish their camping and survival skills.

(Facing page) Snow country will challenge the photographer. (Photo by Ray Stebbins)

169

Generally they set up camp and stay in one area in order to have time for these activities.

PHOTOGRAPHY

Snow country is beautiful. Though its beauty can be enjoyed by anyone, it holds a special appeal for the photographer. The subtle colors, the strange and graceful forms of barren trees and wind-cut drifts, the play of light on crystalline snow all add up to impressive scenic photos. The ever changing elements of a winter landscape offer an exciting challenge to the imaginative camera buff.

Winter also is a prime time for wildlife photography. The animals, more concerned with survival than with man, are far less wary. Many species never seen in summer become highly visible on the winter scene. Truly impressive wildlife shots are often possible in the snow-covered back country.

Cold-weather photography does have its problems. Mainly they involve malfunctions due to cold, lens fogging, film breakage and problems of contrast and exposure due to the high light reflectance of snow.

Cameras

Most cameras work surprisingly well in moderate cold and can be carried without any special precautions. While expensive cameras should be expected to work better in colder temperatures, such is not always the case. Inexpensive models, with a wider tolerance between moving parts, sometimes perform better than the high-priced jobs. Older cameras, for the same reason, often work well in severe cold. My ancient Zeiss is my most dependable cold-weather performer, while a newer and more expensive 35 mm often quits at low temperatures.

Anyone buying a camera specifically for cold-weather use may be interested in the advice given to me by two top professionals, who both recommended the Nikonos, Nikon's

In winter, a plastic bag makes a good camera cover. It not only protects the camera from melting snow but also helps fight condensation. (Photo by Ray Stebbins)

underwater camera. Being moisture proof makes it a very reliable performer in severe cold, they claim.

Usually, I carry my camera in a case, but not inside my jacket. Being outside keeps the camera's temperature closer to that of the air, which reduces problems of condensation. I also cover it with a plastic sack. You'll be amazed at how much snow can get inside a camera case if you fall. If temperatures are very low, however, it's a good idea to carry the camera inside your jacket or parka, in order to keep it warm enough to operate. If you are active, body moisture will condense on lens and eyepiece. A lens cap and case will help, and, if you cover the case with the plastic sack, most of the moisture will be kept out. Also, when you take your camera out to shoot, it may fog up so badly you can't see through the eyepiece. Wiping it off with lens tissue won't help, since the fogging reappears immediately. Even when the camera adjusts to air temperature, the condensation may remain, especially if it's inside. I've found, in this case, that wrapping the camera in extra clothing and leaving it overnight in my pack will sometimes clear it up. Often, however, the cold-weather photographer must simply learn to live with fogging.

Books and articles on the subject sometimes recommend that cameras be winterized for cold-weather shooting. The work must be done by a competent camera repairman. It consists of tearing down the camera completely and removing all traces of lubricant, replacing it with a powdered type or none at all. It is an expensive procedure. Moreover, if you want to use the camera in summer, you'll either have to go to the same expense to have it relubed, or accept a high wear factor and short camera life. Most of the pros I know don't bother, though one has an extra that he had winterized and uses only in cold weather. Mine aren't winterized and I wouldn't recommend it.

Accessories

Light Meters. If kept warm in your pocket, most light meters will work fairly well in cold weather. However, if you do much winter shooting, you'll be better off with a selenium cell type of meter. It has no batteries to fail and it seems to work better in the bright light conditions common to the snow country.

Filters. Filters are a matter of personal technique. At one time I carried all of the standards and, in winter, included one that reduced the blue color of the snow and was supposed to brighten scenes on cloudy days. I didn't like the results. Now I don't take anything except a neutral density filter, which has no effect other than to reduce the amount of light that reaches the film. It's handy for slowing down black-and-white film in bright snow scenes. As far as I am concerned, filters spoil the beautiful effects of winter light.

Lenses and Flash. In addition to the standard 50 mm lens of my

35 mm camera, I generally carry a 28 mm wide angle and a 200 mm telephoto. Battery operated equipment doesn't function in low temperatures, so I don't bother with an electronic flash. You can do a fine job with natural light. I've shot color inside a snow cave using Ektachrome—X and 1/15 and f2, though I did enlarge the cave's air hole for a bit more light.

Equipment Carriers. Since you don't want to set your equipment down in the snow, a handy way to carry accessories is in the pockets of a light fishing vest. It can be worn outside on good days and under your jacket when it's colder. Another useful carrier is the skier's belt pouch, worn with the pouch in front.

Film

Film for the day's shooting should be carried in your inner pockets. In the cold, it tends to get brittle and requires very gentle handling. Be especially careful when loading, unloading, advancing, or rewinding. Always wind very, very slowly to avoid breaking the film and tearing out sprocket holes.

I'd start out with the film you've been using, since you are already familiar with its characteristics. Later, you may want to experiment. For black-and-white, a photographer friend of mine recommends Kodak's Panatomic—X. He uses this very fine grained film to pick up the crystalline structure of the snow. This adds texture to his scenes. The film's slow ASA rating of 32 also makes it a good choice for bright snow shots.

Since I never shoot color for prints, my color film is confined to Ektachrome 64 and Kodachrome 35.

Shooting

To keep from exposing your hands and equipment to the storm and cold any longer than necessary, plan your shots in advance. Don't take out camera or light meter until you have decided on camera angles and framing. If you have a meter, use it to determine settings before uncasing your camera. After you've fogged the eyepiece once, you'll learn to hold your breath while shooting.

With black-and-white film, snow shooting tends to produce contrasty negatives, even on cloudy days. You can help matters in the darkroom by decreasing the developing time of the film. Start by cutting the time ten percent. If the negative is still too dense, then cut it some more.

Because snow reflects a lot of light, exposure can be tricky and you'll need to do plenty of bracketing. Foregrounds, faces, people and animals tend to be underexposed, while snow and backgrounds are often overexposed. You'll probably be using a reflectance meter, or a through the lens meter, which is the same. Take a reading on the light areas and another on the faces or foreground subject. With a spot type meter, you can usually do it where you stand, but with weighted or averaging meters, you'll want to move in close to read the dark areas. Take an average between the two readings. Once you've picked your exposure, bracket. I like to hit at least two half-stops on each side for black-and-white and at least a full stop on each side for color. On general scenic shots, it's better to be a little under than overexposed.

Some interesting effects can be obtained by letting the high contrast work for you. Try silhouetting by exposing for the lightest areas, letting the foreground and figures go black. Color snow scenes, like the black-and-white, often have too much contrast. Therefore, on sunny days, take advantage of the early morning and late evening light. The color effects can be striking. Some of your best color shots will be taken on cloudy days when the winter colors are their most subtle.

In any case, if you are a photographer, you'll enjoy trying to capture the many moods of the winter landscape. You may also want to try your hand at close-up shots of wildlife. The alert camper who travels on skis or snowshoes will often spot animals that he would never see in summer. Those who are seriously interested in wildlife photography can improve their chances for good photos by learning to read tracks and call predators.

CALLING AND TRACKING GAME

In winter, food and forage are often scarce and the wildlife live on short rations until spring. For this reason, you can occasionally lure predators within camera range. Raccoons, foxes, coyotes, and bobcats abound in many sections of the snow country, and in some areas, lynx and wolf as well. Of these, the wolf, fox, and coyote are the easiest to bring within range. The cats tend to be more cautious. But, on occasion, almost any predator can be brought in with the proper call.

Calling

Several years ago, I was camped alone in Wyoming's Snowy Range. While busy with camp chores, I accidentally called in a fox. My waders, rubbing together, squeaked every time I moved. It didn't occur to me that the sound was like that of a squealing rabbit, until the fox suddenly bounded into the middle of my camp. As I stood absolutely still, he trotted about sniffing out the area. He seemed in prime condition. His coat was bright and high colored and his bushy tail, extended and puffed, appeared as large as his body. For several minutes, he searched the camp, ignoring me completely. Finally, convinced that no rabbit dinner was there, the fox stopped directly in front of me, not three feet away. He gave me a look that, if translated into words, would surely have been unprintable. Then, he calmly trotted off. Fascinated by his antics, I had completely forgotten the camera dangling around my neck.

That experience convinced me that calling game couldn't be too difficult, so I ordered a set of calls from the Burnham Brothers of Marble Falls, Texas. The set consisted of two reed type calls. One was a long-range job used to attract the predator and the other a short-range call for teasing the animals in close. Along with them, I purchased a practice record so I'd know just how the calls should sound. Working with them was much easier than using a duck or turkey call.

The technique of calling is fairly simple. Once you are in the

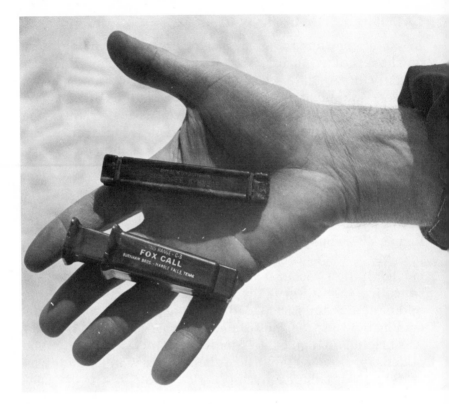

Predator calls used to attract animals that feed on rabbits. On top is the short-range call and on the bottom the long-range call. (Photo by Ray Stebbins)

back country, hide in a brushy spot where you have a good view of the surrounding area. The wind should be blowing into your face or quartering, and never from behind your back. With snow on the ground, it's handy to have an old bedsheet along. You can throw it over you and blend into the scenery almost anywhere.

Once you've settled in a spot, blow the long-range call, maybe six or eight times. Wait a moment or two and blow again. Continue to space out six or so calls at intervals of several minutes. When you spot an animal, switch to the short-range call. Don't blow it when the animal is looking in your direction, but each time he looks away, give two short squeals. Keep this up until you've teased him into camera range.

Try one area for at least ten minutes and, if there is no action, move half a mile or a mile and try again. It does take patience. On several occasions, I've quit too soon and run into the predator as I left my place of concealment.

You'll find it's fun to play Pied Piper to the local wildlife, even if you are not a photographer. Calling up wild animals to near eyeball confrontation is exciting.

Tracking

Larger animals that inhabit the back country, such as deer, elk, and moose, are easy to track in the snow. The photographer who takes good photos of game animals often employs the same tactics as the hunter. Actually, he must do a better job of tracking. It is much easier to get within rifle range of game than to get within camera range, for even with a telephoto lens, you must be up close. Tracking is one way to get there.

Anyone who has spent much time in the back country should be familiar with various animal signs. If you're not, I'd recommend reading Ernest Thompson Seton's old classic, *Animal Tracks and Hunter Signs*. In areas where there is enough game to make tracking worthwhile, you'll undoubtedly see plenty of tracks. The decision to follow a set will depend on how fresh they appear. It is difficult to judge accurately, but with a little experience, you can make a reasonable guess. Check to see if the tracks are sharp-edged and clean; that is, see if any snow or debris has been blown into them. The small ridge of snow, formed by the space between the hoof, should be visible, while the snow disturbed by the dragging of the toe, should be sharply crystalline.

Normally, game animals move from bedding areas to feeding grounds in the early morning and late evening. That's when most tracks are made. In winter, however, fodder is so scarce that many animals will feed in open meadows, if undisturbed, until late in the morning. Then they often move

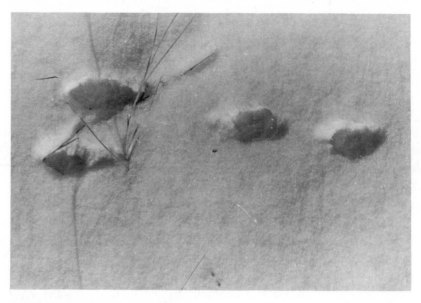

Rabbit tracks are easy to spot in the snow. These tracks belong to a cotton-tail. (Photo by Ray Stebbins)

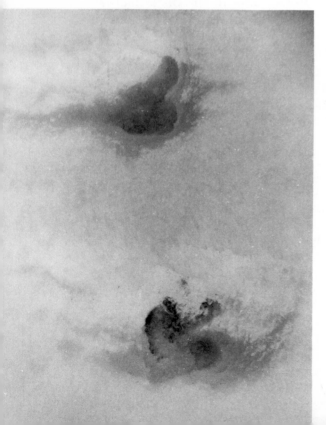

Here are the tracks of a young mule deer. (Photo by Ray Stebbins)

back to the bedding area slowly, browsing on the way. Of course, it's easier to spot and to approach a feeding animal.

Unless the cover is particularly good, it's often best to approach the animal openly rather than trying to sneak up on him. The chance of frightening the game into panicked flight is reduced. But don't walk directly toward the animal; approach at a wide, oblique angle. Stay downwind, of course, and never move when the creature has his head up. Wait until he lowers it to feed. Close in very slowly and don't make any sudden movements. He may move out, but usually he will do so slowly. Never deliberately spook an animal. Forcing him to run costs him energy that he can ill afford to spare in winter.

The efforts you expend in tracking and calling game can result in excellent photos. It can also develop your awareness

Mule deer peer at the cameraman. Game is generally less spooky in winter and hence easier to stalk with a camera. (Photo courtesy of the Montana Department of Highways)

and knowledge of wildlife. Some campers, however, are already dedicated to another outdoor activity. They'd rather go fishing.

ICE FISHING

Most states and provinces now permit year-round fishing, or at least offer a winter season, and many anglers have extended their sport through the winter months. It makes an ideal activity for the winter camper.

Equipment for ice fishing needn't be elaborate or expensive. Even a fishing pole isn't an absolute requirement, and some anglers simply use a handline. I prefer a short, inexpensive jigging pole. They are about a foot long, are equipped with a plastic reel to hold the line, and include a spring device that when triggered, gives the tip of the pole a sharp flip. This causes the bait or lure to jig up and down, which is supposed to attract the fish. However, almost any type of rig will do for ice fishing.

The line you use should be stout. Some anglers prefer a squid line that tests to thirty pounds. In my area, a popular line is a seventeen to twenty pound monofil. The purpose of a heavy line is to avoid wearing it through against the sharp edges of the ice at the bottom of the hole. An active fish can saw through a light line very quickly.

The best way to select baits and lures is to talk to the local fishermen. They can often tell you about special tricks, lures and baits that seem to work best in their waters. Many times, however, the camper will be going into areas that are seldom fished in winter. In such a case, I like to rely on natural baits such as worms, nightcrawlers or, where permitted, small minnows. Live bait should be kept in an insulated container to keep it from freezing. Along with the bait, I'll take a chunk of soft, yellow cheese. Though it may sound strange, cheese is a popular bait in many areas and is well worth trying when other lures fail to produce.

Fishing through the ice attracts many anglers to winter camping. (Photo by Ray Stebbins)

Some artificial lures are also popular. Many anglers like to use small spoons or wobblers in various color combinations, red and white being among the most common. They feel that jigging such a lure acts as an attractor to bring the fish in to the bait. Ice flies are common in some areas. They are usually tied on a number four- to six-size hook weighted with lead foil. Most consist of a hair or heavy chenille body and long tail hackles of the same color. Black, white, yellow, and orange seem to be the most popular colors. One of my favorite winter lures is the maribou jig in solid colors of yellow, black, and orange. But the best advice on lures is simply to take a variety and experiment to see what works best.

You also will need to take an auger or spud for making holes in the ice and a large sieve or perforated ladle to scoop the ice chips out of the hole. When backpacking, we usually take a spoon-bladed auger since it is lighter than the worm-bladed types. Most augers drill a six-, seven-, or eight-inch hole, which is large enough for most game fish. For chopping larger holes, anglers use a spud — a long, steel bar with a chisel-type blade on one end and a T-bar handle on the other. A cord is tied to the handle and goes around the fisherman's wrist. It prevents him from dropping the bar into the hole as he chops through the ice.

Finding the right depth at which to fish is an important part of the technique. There are exceptions, of course, but most ice fishing in lakes is probably done at depths of twenty to thirty feet. Generally, it's best to start your fishing just off bottom. I like to let my sinker touch down, then reel up one or two turns. If, after a reasonable wait, there is no action, I'll reel up several feet, keeping track of the number of turns of the reel. Then, at intervals, I'll continue to take up the line until I find the level where the fish seem to be working.

In new areas, always be careful when going out on the ice, especially on lakes that are snow covered. The snow can insulate the ice and produce thin spots, or by forcing water up through the cracks, make rotten ice, which, even when thick, won't hold much weight.

For many campers, developing skill as an ice fisherman is a fun way to spend time in the winter wilderness. Some claim that such knowledge is a valuable survival tool. Under certain circumstances, I suppose it might be. However, the surest way to survival is through the development of winter camping skills.

PRACTICING SURVIVAL

One of the most practical and valuable ways of spending time in the winter wilderness is in practicing survival skills. In fact, anyone who enjoys winter camping and spends much time at it, should be familiar with the basics of survival. I've never known an outdoorsman, even among professional guides I've met, who hasn't been lost at one time or another. If you spend enough time in the back country, the odds will eventually overtake you. In most cases it works out all right and within a day or two at the most, you either find your way out or are found. Yet, for that day or so, you must survive.

In an earlier chapter, we discussed panic and how hard it is to control, yet how important it is to remain calm. To do so requires a solid belief in your ability to handle the situation. In fact, experts on the subject maintain that one of the most important factors in successful survival is confidence. If you know from previous practice that you can make it in the winter wilderness with only matches and a knife, the odds are all in your favor.

So, during your trips to the snow country, it would be well worth the time to practice building shelters, making fires under adverse conditions, and developing a sensible survival kit that suits you. A good way to begin is by going alone into an isolated, but, preferably, a familiar area. Assume that you are lost, separated from your equipment, and that you have only a knife and a fire kit.

Shelters

Lost and facing at least one cold, long night in the back country, the natural impulse is to hustle up a wagon load of wood and build a fire. A man alone, however, can't tend a fire and build a shelter at the same time. In most cases, a shelter should come first. In summer, a campfire may see you through, but the winter camper usually needs protection from wind and snow if he is to survive.

Snow Pits. If there is snow on the ground at least three feet deep, you can build a snow pit more quickly than any other shelter. The easiest way is to find a large fir or spruce with dense, lower branches that are close to or touching the snow. With a long stick, knock the snow off the branches all around, and as high up as you can reach. Then, in a survival situation, you would use your skis, snowshoes or a forked stick to dig out the snow at the base of the tree. When only practicing, I'd take along a knock-down snowshovel, to save wear and tear on your equipment.

Dig out a pit large enough to sit in comfortably with your head below the top edge and your shoulders clear of the sides. With your legs straight out, there should be enough room at the far end for a small fire. Then, clear a place for storing firewood, either in the shelter or under the branches of the tree.

When the pit is finished, line the bottom and wall, against which you'll be leaning, with something that will insulate you from the snow. If you sit or lie down on the snow itself, body warmth will melt it immediately and you end up wet and chilled. In an actual survival situation, you could use anything available for lining the bottom and back wall of the pit. In practice, use only dead limbs or deadfall rather than cut boughs or bark from a living tree.

To complete the shelter, build a platform for a fire at the far end of the pit. You may have to trim some of the branches just above the fireplace to let the smoke out. Keep the fire small so there is no danger of setting the tree ablaze.

A snow pit can be dug out in the open and roofed over with branches, deadfall, or blocks of snow. Whatever the roof is made of, it should be packed with loose snow to increase the insulating efficiency of the shelter. Obviously, if you can find a good tree, it will save you time and effort.

A well made snow pit will keep you reasonably warm in all but the most severe weather. In fact, in 1974, a thirteen-year-old Boy Scout survived two nights of sub-freezing cold in a Montana wilderness in just this type of shelter. Even though he didn't have a fire the second night, he came through in fine shape.

Snow Caves and Burrows. Digging a snow cave or burrow usually takes longer and entails more work, but under certain conditions, it is the better choice. It takes advantage of the excellent insulating properties of the snow, so it is the safest shelter to use when temperatures are extremely low and winds are high.

A snow cave or burrow starts with a tunnel dug into the base of a drift. Note that the excavator is wearing rain gear in order to stay dry. (Photo by Ray Stebbins)

The difference between a burrow and a snow cave is merely a matter of complexity. A burrow is just that, a hole in the snow just large enough to hold a man lying down. It is, in fact, much like the burrow of an animal and is used for the same purpose. Snow caves are larger, roomier, and more comfortable.

Regardless of which you dig, it is difficult to keep dry unless temperatures are low, and yet it is extremely important to stay as dry as possible. When you start, keep boughs, or bark under your knees to keep them from soaking up snow melt. Make the entrance to the shelter large enough so that you are not constantly rubbing against the walls. Try to keep the snow brushed off your clothing. Once you have hollowed out some working room inside the drift, it will be warm enough inside so that you can remove some outer clothing. Take off as much as you need to insure that much will stay dry. Even then, pace yourself to avoid excessive sweating. Getting wet and chilled can be as dangerous as having no shelter at all.

To dig a burrow, you'll need to find a snowbank several feet high. Clear out a tunnel at the base of the bank, about two or three feet long. The tunnel entrance should be, as nearly as possible, at right angles to the prevailing wind direction to keep it from being covered by drifting snow. Enlarge the end of the tunnel so that you can work inside the snowbank.

Then, dig out a chamber large enough to allow you to stretch out full length. It should be parallel to the long axis of the drift and dug so that the outer wall is at least a foot thick. The sleeping area should be a foot or two higher than the tunnel floor to discourage cold air from drifting into the shelter. You can hollow out as much headroom as energy and inclination permit. For ventilation, poke a hole through the wall with a stick, ski pole or snowshoe tail. Then under actual survival conditions, you would line the sleeping area with thick layers of evergreen boughs to provide comfort and insulation.

The design of snowcaves is limited only by the endurance and imagination of the camper. Paul Pedzoldt, famous mountaineer and head of the National Outdoor Leadership School,

uses snow caves on his annual midwinter assault on Wyoming's Grand Teton Peak. One year, an assistant leader,
Lawrence Higby, supervised the digging of a cave that
consisted of a foyer and four rooms, complete with bridal
suite. It was dubbed "Higby's Hilton."

You don't need a cave that elaborate, but you should build at
least one. On a trip where we plan to be in one area for several
days and where we know the snow will be deep, my partner
and I often use a snow cave. In this case, the tent is left at home
and is replaced in the pack by a break-down snow shovel along
with a Space Blanket or waterproof nylon tarp.

On arriving at our campsite, we find a large drift, well over
head high. We peel off some outer clothing, put on our
waterproof gear, and start to dig.

To speed the digging, we place the Space Blanket or tarp on
the floor of the tunnel. One man, digging inside, piles the snow
on the blanket. The other camper, outside, hauls the blanket
load of snow out and dumps it.

First, we tunnel into the base of the drift for several feet. At
the end of the tunnel, we hollow out a circular area high enough
so that we can stand up. Then, parallel to the long axis of the
snowbank, we dig out a large sleeping chamber with plenty of
floor room for two bedrolls. We start this digging about waist
high, which places the floor of the sleeping area several feet
above the level of the entrance, so that the cold air will settle in
the tunnel. The area above the sleeping platform is dug out
high enough to allow us to sit up comfortably. This chamber
comprises one end of the cave. In the middle, opposite the
tunnel, we dig back a small area for a kitchen and on the other
end of the cave, we hollow out a large shelf for our packs and
gear. Except for skis or snowshoes, we will bring everything
into the cave so that it won't be covered by snowfall and lost.

When the cave is finished, we use our ski poles to poke two
air vents in the outer wall, one above the sleeping area and
another opposite the cooking area. For a final touch, in the
inner wall, we cut out a small shelf for a candle. The sleeping
area is covered with the Space Blanket or tarp to provide

insulation from the snow. Our bedding goes over that.

On the average, it will take four and a half to five hours of fairly steady work to dig a cave this size. You can, of course, hollow out a smaller but adequate cave in two or three hours. Once you've tried it, however, you'll probably go for the larger model.

Even in severe cold, the temperature inside a snow cave or burrow will stay around 32 degrees F. In the still air, it is quite comfortable and generally much warmer than a tent. Cooking, or even a single candle, will raise the temperature, but don't allow the temperature to remain above freezing any longer than necessary, because the roof will start to drip. For this reason, it's a good idea, while cooking, to keep your bedding rolled up. If you use the same cave for several days, the roof may begin to sag. It's no problem, just shave off enough snow to keep it the height you want.

All considerations of survival aside, every outdoorsman owes it to himself to spend at least one night of his life in a snow cave. Sleeping in a snow cave has been described as a return to the womb, an Oz-trip, or, simply, "far out." All of which means that it's an experience hard to describe. Outside the wind may howl and scream, the lightning crash, and the heavens thunder, but inside the cave there is absolute quiet. Not a sound from the "other world" can penetrate its walls. For perhaps the first time, you may enjoy the strange sensation of utter silence.

In addition, building a snow cave seems to satisfy some primitive urge to conquer the hostile environment — in style. In short, there is no other outdoor experience quite like it.

The Lean-to. It's possible, of course, to be lost in an area where there is no snow, or where it isn't deep enough even to dig a burrow. In this case, a lean-to can be the answer.

One often thinks of a lean-to in terms of those neat, roomy shelters depicted in camping books. Actually, it can be a shelter of any kind, closed on all but one side, which is left open to a warming fire. It can be made of rocks, brush, or deadfall.

Here is an elaborate snow cave with several chambers. (Photo courtesy of Milt McLaskey and Dana Van Burgh)

More often, it is a framework of poles, covered with evergreen boughs, bark, tree limbs, or anything that will turn wind and snow.

Normally, you would lash the poles together with parachute cord and, perhaps, cover them with a plastic sheet. However, if you are practicing survival, you'll assume that you have no equipment other than a knife and matches. This means you'll have to improvise a frame that is self-supporting.

Start by selecting a sturdy ridge pole, at least twelve feet long, preferably a standing, dead sapling (in an emergency, of course, you could cut down a living tree). Don't trim off the limbs flush with the trunk; leave stubs of several inches, which will serve to hold the rest of the frame.

Prop one end of the ridge pole against a firm support, such as the crotch of a standing tree, placing it so that you can sit up comfortably under the high end. Select a dozen or more smaller poles that can be trimmed so that there are plenty of short stubs left on them. Lean these against the ridge pole at intervals of two feet or so, and at an angle of about forty-five degrees. You'll end up with a framework that looks like the skeleton of a fish with the ridge pole, the backbone and the smaller poles, the ribs.

Next, lay trimmed branches on the stubs of the smaller poles, so that they are roughly parallel to the ground. Starting at the bottom, as though you were shingling a roof, cover these cross poles with a thick thatch of evergreen boughs, by cutting a stub at the butt end of the bough and hanging it on the cross pole. When practicing, cut only a few boughs just to see how it's done. Don't damage trees unnecessarily.

The open side of the lean-to should face away from the prevailing wind. If possible, locate the entrance so that a fire built in front of it will be clear of overhanging branches. You don't want snow to drop from the tree and put out a survival fire. The lean-to can be any size you like, but as a minimum it should be high enough to allow you to sit up comfortably in the entrance and several feet longer than your stretched-out body. Clear snow off the floor and cover the whole floor with a thick bed of boughs.

You'll save time and effort if you can find something that will serve as one wall of the shelter, or that will take the place of the ridge pole. A large, downed tree will often provide most of the framework. By merely trimming out a few of the underside branches, you will have the beginnings of a good shelter. Or, perhaps you can find a large boulder that will serve as one wall. By leaning the rib poles against it, you can also eliminate the ridge pole. The tangle of dirt and rocks that cling to the roots of a fallen tree will sometimes work as well as a boulder. There are, of course, many improvisations. Generally, a man's imagination will be stimulated by a survival situation, if he remains calm.

Warmth and Sustenance

In addition to a shelter, you will need warmth and something
to drink. With these three necessities alone, you can survive
for several weeks in the winter wilderness. Certainly this is
long enough to be found by searchers in most every case. If you
have fire-starting materials, warmth should be no problem,
especially if you've been practicing building fires with damp
wood. Water should be available, at least in the form of snow
or ice.

With the addition of food, survival could be extended
indefinitely, but unless you're luckier than a sweepstakes
winner, chances are slim that you'll do much eating. There is
food available in the winter wilderness. Plants, small animals
and fish are found the year round in snow country. The big
hitch is not the difficulty·in collecting them but doing so in
sufficient quantities to make it worthwhile.

I've spent many years in the outdoors, including some time
as a professional hunting and fishing guide. There are a fair
number of edible plants and mushrooms that I can readily
identify. Yet, it's doubtful that I could gather much food in the
winter wilderness, equipped only with matches and a knife. It
may be fun to try when it isn't a matter of life and death. But
survival is a matter of *net* calories. Even if you were successful
in getting food, chances are it wouldn't begin to replace the
calories you lost collecting it. This means that after the effort
of getting the food and eating it, you'd end up weaker than you
would have been without it.

It's true that most survival kits include materials for
making snares and for fishing. Yet even in summer, the
usefulness of these items is limited. In winter, they are
generally worthless. The fishing items might conceivably
help, but, in most cases, it would be difficult to hack through
several feet of ice to make a hole and unlikely that you'd get
enough fish to replace the calories it cost to do so. As for snares,
very few men can handle them effectively. Even experienced
trappers will have difficulty when their traps are replaced by a
piece of parachute cord or a chunk of picture frame wire. So,

even if the camper were knowledgeable about small game, fish, and flora, it's unlikely his efforts would pay off in terms of net calories gained. Therefore, in most cases, the winter survivor is better off staying in his camp, keeping warm and conserving his energy to signal for help.

Signaling

Under survival conditions, signaling is generally confined to fires, noise, and perhaps an SOS stomped out in the snow. The other types of signaling devices such as flares, chemical smoke, mirrors, and whistles won't be available to a man lost without his equipment.

Thus, in a survival situation, your camp should always be located on the edge of a large clearing or a large, solidly frozen lake. Since much of the searching today is done by aircraft, you'll want to do your signaling from the center of an open area where you can be spotted from the air. In the center of the clearing, carefully lay a fire that can be lit quickly. To protect it from wet and snow, cover it with evergreen boughs. You'll need them in any case. For once the fire is started, you'll want to add the green stuff to make as much smoke as possible. In emergencies, a single evergreen tree, in an open area can be set afire to attract the attention of searchers. Since it's a one shot deal, never set fire to the tree until you actually hear or see the aircraft.

Some survival manuals and camping books include a page of emergency ground-to-air signals. You are generally instructed to stomp them out in the snow in twenty-foot letters. It seems pointless, however, to learn that an upside down, doubled barred T means, "Have sprained Achilles tendon — drop aspirin." It won't hurt, of course, to stomp out a large SOS in the clearing. You can line the letters with bark, boughs, or whatever, to make them stand out against the snow. Even a pilot no brighter than your brother-in-law can figure out that you are in trouble.

If you have reason to believe that a ground search has

started, you can make noise. Shouting won't do much more than wear out your voice. A better way is to bang on a rock, tree, or hollow log with a solid stick. Strike three times, wait an interval and repeat the procedure. A series of three of anything is the universal distress signal.

Survival Kits

Once you have done some practicing of survival techniques, you're ready to design your personal survival kit. Most commercial kits are poorly planned and seldom adequate for winter use. One exception is the snowmobiler's kit put out by Survival Systems Incorporated (see appendix). It's a good kit, but even here I'd make some changes. The fact is, you won't want to take anyone else's selection without checking it to see if it suits you. A kit should contain the items that you have personally chosen because you know they are necessary and will work.

Of course, ski tourers and snowshoers traveling with a backpack won't need a kit unless they somehow become separated from their pack gear. That shouldn't happen. And if it did, any kit large enough to be of any use would have to have been carried in the pack and would be lost along with it.

Snowmobilers and anyone taking trips out of a base camp with a day pack should carry some emergency gear. For a container to hold the survival items, you'll want something that is useful itself. Most campers take some type of metal container, often an aluminum sandwich box with tight-fitting lid. The box serves as a cooking pot to melt drinking water and to make soups or hot drinks. Another useful container is a cardboard box that has been soaked in melted paraffin. It can double as a fire starter. A small, heavy duty, aluminum-foil cake pan folded flat will serve as cooking gear.

In addition, you'll need a minimum of survival food, high energy, for the most part. Mine usually includes a Wilson's meat bar, three one-ounce bars of Hershey's tropical chocolate, and four to six bouillon cubes.

Author's survival kit consists of (left row, top to bottom) a 12-ounce container, 50 feet of nylon twine, compass and knife, survival blanket of Mylar Foil; (middle row, top to bottom) plastic lid for container, wire saw, bouillon cubes, metal match and matches in plastic bag, combo fire starter and tinder, and candle; (right row, top to bottom) whistle, signal mirror, three chocolate bars (450 calories), and a bacon bar (480 calories). (Photo by Ray Stebbins)

To insure that there will be plenty of wood for a survival fire, I always include a wire saw. It is an inexpensive tool, available from most suppliers. It rolls into a small circle that takes up very little space. It consists of two heavy sawtooth wires fitted with finger rings at each end. It will easily saw through a six-inch log. When using it, however, take it slow and easy, since overheating will quickly wear it out.

Every winter survival kit should include an emergency Space Rescue Blanket. It is merely a blanket-sized piece of thin Mylar foil that folds up small enough to fit in the palm of your hand. It reflects body heat, providing warmth and insulation from the snow. I also like to take two large plastic sacks of the kind used for garbage or leaf bags. They can be used as wet gear, to keep you dry while digging a snow cave, and for additional insulation from the snow.

My own kit includes fifty feet of heavy nylon cord and, of course, a fire kit, which consists of a candle stub, matches, fire starter, and a Metal Match. It also contains an extra compass and a small pocket knife. Fortunately, I haven't yet had to use any signal equipment, but my kit includes a signaling mirror, a whistle, and a chemical smoke device about the size of a 35 mm film can. Except for the signal gear, I've used all of the other items at one time or another. They work for me and I have confidence in the kit.

Yet I'm sure that many campers wouldn't agree entirely with my selections. Your own experience is the best guide. When you've assembled your kit, try it out so you will know what it will do for you.

Of course, the best way to survive is to never get into a survival situation. If you do, however, remember that making it with a minimum of equipment is a matter of staying calm, staying confident, staying warm, and staying put.

8

Where to Go

Anyone who lives in Canada or in the snow belt states of the United States isn't far from good winter camping. In addition to the many private facilities now available year-round, there are thousands of acres of public lands open to the cold-weather camper. In the United States, the national forests and parks, state parks, state forests, and national recreation areas offer a great variety of campsites.

In the East and Midwest, tent camping tends to be more closely regulated, but winter facilities for the RV camper are more readily available there than in the West. Western states do have an advantage in that many national forests and wilderness areas are located there. Generally they provide almost unrestricted winter camping. Some forest areas, however, do have regulations governing winter use and it is best to check with the local forest supervisor before planning a trip. The addresses of Forest Service offices for the snow belt areas are given below. Not all national parks are open in winter, but those that are offer some spectacular attractions.

Canada has long been known as a winter playground and its facilities — both public and private — for the ski tourer, snowshoer, and snowmobiler are well developed. An extensive system of provincial parks and forests, and national parks and preserves provide thousands of winter campsites. As in the U.S., camping near the more populous centers tends to be highly regulated, but most provinces offer plenty of wilderness areas where the more adventurous winter sportsman can break his own trails.

In all states and provinces, snowmobiling is regulated and it is advisable to check current rules and requirements before making plans.

Information on nearby areas often can be obtained from local skiers and snowmobilers. Since many of them are winter campers, they are responsible, in great part, for the rapid development of cold-weather camping. It was for them that government agencies began plowing rural roads and clearing parking areas from which winter campers now take off into the back country.

More detailed information can be obtained free from state and provincial tourist bureaus, which are paying more attention to the needs of winter campers these days. The influx of snow sportsmen has been the salvation of some communities that normally died each winter. Many resort areas, once hard pressed because they depended on a short summer season, are now healthy, year-round concerns. A winter camper is as welcome as a Christmas bonus, almost everywhere.

So, if you don't already have an area in mind, I'd suggest you contact your local state or provincial tourist office. They can provide copies of regulations, trail maps of ski and snowmobile areas, as well as lists of campgrounds, both public and private, that remain open year-round.

Due to the ever-increasing number of such areas, it would be impossible to list them all or cover them in any great detail. However, this chapter contains addresses and summaries of selected areas. It will give you some idea of the many opportunities available.

THE EASTERN UNITED STATES

Connecticut. Write to the State of Connecticut, Department of Environmental Protection, State Office Building, Hartford 06115. Connecticut is fortunate in having a well-developed state forest system. It provides for snowmobiling, ski touring, and camping in all areas of the state. These winter sports are regulated and a list of forests open to each activity, as well as trail maps, can be obtained from the Department of Environmental Protection. Last season, eleven forests were open to snowmobiling. A fee and registration of machines are required. Recommended areas for cross country skiing are found in both forests and state parks throughout the region. Organized winter camping is found in Macedonia Brook State Park, Kettletown State Park, Cockaponset State Forest and at Pachang State Forest. Sites are available on a first-come basis. There is a fee of two dollars for off-season camping.

Maine. Write to Maine Department of Commerce and Industry, State House, Augusta 04330. For information on wilderness areas, contact the Maine Forestry Department, and to check snowmobile regulations, write the Department of Inland Fisheries and Game, both at the above address. Some 3,000 miles of U.S. Highways and 22,000 miles of secondary roads in the state are kept plowed, open, and sanded in all weather, year-round. And for snowmobilers, ski tourers, and campers, there are state and federal parks open all year. Some of these offer relatively deluxe camping for tenters and RV owners. There also are wilderness areas, including the famous Allagash, which provides several hundred square miles of primitive back country.

Acadia National Park offers a unique experience for the winter sportsman. Its 42,000 acres are almost entirely surrounded by the sea. It is accessible all year via Maine highway 3, from Ellsworth to Hull's Cove entrance. Areas for ski touring, snowshoeing and snowmobiling are provided and there is winter camping at Blackwoods Campground. The park is open throughout the winter season, December to April.

For details, write to the Superintendent, Acadia National Park, Hulls Cove 04644.

Massachusetts. Write to Massachusetts Department of Tourism, Box 1775, Boston 02105. Snowmobilers should write to Massachusetts Division of Marine Recreation, 64 Causeway Street, Boston 02114, and for additional camping information, contact the Appalachian Mountain Clubs, 5 Jay Street, Boston 02108. There are areas for ski touring, snowmobiling, and camping throughout the state in ninety state parks and forests. During the winter season, Labor Day to the last Saturday in June, there is no limit on camping days, but camping must be done in designated areas. In addition, some sixty private campgrounds are open through the winter season.

New Hampshire. Write to New Hampshire Division of Economic Development, Box 856, Concord 03301. For snowmobile information, contact the Bureau of Off-Highway Vehicles, at the same address. There are thirty-four major ski areas, many of which provide ski touring and snowmobiling. Designated camping is permitted in some thirty-four state parks during the winter season. Of the private campgrounds, thirty-four are open year-round, provided facilities for tent and RV campers in all regions of the state.

In the White Mountain National Forest, there are thirty campgrounds, most of which can be used year-round though they are not serviced during winter. For specific information, write to the Forest Supervisor, White Mountain National Forest, Laconia 02346.

New York. Write to the State of New York, Department of Commerce, Travel Bureau, 99 Washington Avenue, Albany 12210. New York state has a vast amount of land open to winter recreation. More than 100 communities offer areas for snowmobiling and up-to-date information on conditions is available from the toll free number, 800-234-5110. Registration is handled by the District Offices of the Motor Vehicle

Division and information on regulations is available from the Division of Marine and Recreational Vehicles, South Mall, Albany 12223. There are ninety-six major ski areas, covering every region of the state. Dozens of public and private campgrounds are open in winter for the tent and RV campers. And primitive camping is permitted on most state lands in the state reforestation areas and forest preserves. Check with the Bureau of Forest Recreation, New York Department of Environmental Conservation, 50 Wolf Road, Albany 12205.

Pennsylvania. Write to the Office of Public Information, Department of Environmental Resources, Harrisburg 17120. In addition to private campgrounds, Pennsylvania has forty-four state parks. Of these, twenty-six remain open during the winter season, October through April. Other public campgrounds permit winter camping where sanitary facilities are operable and when weather permits. Access, however, is not assured, so check with the park superintendent before making plans.

The 74,000-acre Allegheny National Forest offers ten hiking trails, including a part of the Appalachian Trail. For camping information, write to the Forest Supervisor, Allegheny National Forest, Warren 16365.

Vermont. Write to the Agency of Environmental Conservation, Montpelier 05602. All state lands, forests, and parks are open to ski touring and snowshoeing. Certain state parks and forests have been designated for snowmobile use. Camping areas on state lands are not closed during winter, but roads may not be plowed. Check before planning.

The 240,000-acre Green Mountain National Forest runs nearly two-thirds the length of the state. Areas for ski touring, snowshoeing, and snowmobiling are provided and roads are kept open. No space reservations are required for winter camping. For details, contact the Forest Supervisor, Green Mountain National Forest, 151 West Street, Rutland 05701.

THE MIDWEST

Indiana. Write to the Indiana Tourist Division, 333 State House, Indianapolis 46204. There are fourteen state fish and wildlife areas, thirteen state parks, eleven state recreation areas and ten state forests. In addition, there are more than 150 private campgrounds, Of this total, nearly half remain open year-round. The facilities they provide range from the plush to the primitive.

Iowa. Write to the State Conservation Commission, State Office Building, 300 Fourth Street, Des Moines 50319. The public land in Iowa includes state parks, forests, and recreation areas. They are open seven days a week throughout the winter. The Conservation Commission also manages 25,000 acres of public hunting areas where camping usually is permitted. For details, contact the commission.

Michigan. Write to the Michigan Tourist Council, Suite 102, 300 South Capitol Avenue, Lansing 48962. Michigan claims the greatest amount of snowfall of any winter sports area in the United States, and its provisions for winter activities are impressive. The state is well provided with public lands. An excellent state park and recreation system comprises some 205,000 acres, and four national forests add another two and a half million acres of public land.

Snowmobilers are welcome in most of the state parks and recreation areas and in some areas of the national forests. With private and public facilities combined, there are 162 marked snowmobile areas, covering all regions of the state. There are sixty-seven major ski areas, and some 159 private and public campgrounds are open through the winter season. National forest campgrounds may be used in winter, though no facilities are provided. For camping information, write to the Forest Supervisor of: Huron National Forest, Cadillac 49601; Manistee National Forest, at the same address; Ottawa National Forest, Ironwood 49938; or Hiawatha National Forest, Escanaba 49829.

Minnesota. Write to the State of Minnesota, Department of Natural Resources, Centennial Office Building, St. Paul 55155. The state of Minnesota has more than 3,440 miles of marked snowmobile trails on state, federal, and county lands and 1,400 miles were added last season. Cross country skiing and snowshoeing is permitted in all state parks and forests. Twenty of the state parks are restricted to non-motorized use. There also are hundreds of miles of logging roads on public lands that provide plenty of room for those who want to get away from crowds and camp in solitude. In addition to private campgrounds, twenty state parks are open for winter camping and among the best of these are Savannah Portage Primitive Area, Crosby-Manitou State Park, William O'Brien State Park, Whitewater, and St. Croix State Parks.

Minnesota has two national forests that offer winter action. For information write to Forest Supervisor, Chippewa National Forest, Cass Lake 56633, or to Superior National Forest, Federal Building, Duluth 55801.

North Dakota. Write the North Dakota Highway Department, Capitol Grounds, Bismarck 58501. Snowmobiling is permitted in state parks, in some areas of the national forests, in state forests, and in most game management areas. Trail maps are available from area supervisors. Winter camping is encouraged in those state parks that remain open in winter. Lake Metigoshe State Park, Bottineau Winter Park, and the Theodore Roosevelt National Park are open year-round and are among the best areas for winter activities.

Ohio. Write to Ohio Department of Natural Resources, Division of Forests and Preserves, Fountain Square, Columbus 43224. Ohio's sixty-two state parks are open throughout the winter season. Snowmobiles may be operated in state parks on designated trails; for information on regulations, write the Division of Parks and Recreation at the above address. Hiking trails are provided on state lands for ski tourers and snowshoers. Many state campgrounds have been winterized and are equipped with heated washrooms and electricity.

RV campers enjoy winter facilities at Ohio's Punderson State Park. (Photo courtesy of the Ohio Department of Natural Resources)

The Vesuvius Area of the Wayne National Forest also is open year-round. For information contact the Wayne National Forest, District Ranger, 710 Park Street, Ironton 45638.

Wisconsin. Write the Department of Natural Resources, Box 450, Madison 53701. This is prime snowmobile, snowshoe, and ski touring country. Miles of trails for these activities are provided by fifty-seven state parks and ten state forests. Camping is permitted, without charge, in all state camping areas from October 31 through April 1st. Camping permits are not required after December 1st. Twenty-eight counties own 2,500,000 acres of forest lands, most of which are open for cross country skiing and for snowmobiling, on designated trails. Information and maps are available from the county administration at the courthouse of each county seat.

There are nearly one and a half million acres in the state's two national forests, the Chequamegon and the Nicolet, both of which are open for winter activities. For details, write the U.S. Forest Service, Regional Office, 633 West Wisconsin Avenue, Milwaukee 53203.

THE ROCKY MOUNTAINS

Colorado. Write to Colorado Visitor's Bureau, 225 West Colfax Avenue, Denver 80202. The state is covered by snowmobile trails and the Visitor's Bureau will send you a list of the thirty-nine areas they consider the best in the state. Snowshoeing and cross country skiing are popular activities throughout Colorado and more than a dozen organizations offer group trips and instructions. Most of these are located at or near the major ski areas. A list and description of these organizations also can be obtained from the bureau. Since Colorado is a year-round tourist area, roads are generally kept open, but severe weather can close the high mountain passes. It's always best to check road conditions before traveling.

The state has ten national forests containing over 13,500,000 acres of public land. Where accessible, they offer almost unrestricted snowshoeing, ski touring, and primitive camping. For information, write the U.S. Forest Service, Regional Office, Denver Federal Center, Building 85, Denver 80225.

Rocky Mountain National Park is open all year. Ski touring and snowmobile trails are provided. Tourers making overnight trips must obtain permits. Organized camping is permitted in the Moriane Park Area. For details, contact the Superintendent, Rocky Mountain National Park, Estes Park 80517.

Idaho. Write the Idaho Division of Commerce and Development, Statehouse, Boise 83720. There are twenty-five major ski resorts in Idaho, including some of the oldest and best known in the West.

The real challenge for the winter camper, however, is found

View of the Mt. Evans-Echo Lake country near Denver, Colorado. (Photo courtesy of the Colorado Department of Public Relations)

Dog sled trips are becoming popular in some areas of the snow country. (Photo courtesy of the Colorado Department of Public Relations)

in the twelve national forests, which contain over 20,500,000 acres. They provide unlimited opportunity for touring, snow-mobiling, and camping. For information, write the U.S. Forest Service, Regional Office, Federal Building, Missoula, Montana 59801.

Cross-country skiing at the Big Mountain Area near Whitefish, Montana.
(Photo courtesy of the Montana Department of Highways)

Montana. Write the Montana Highway Department, Travel
Promotion Unit, Helena 59601. There are twenty-seven major
ski areas in the state, most of which offer ski touring and
instructions. Included among them is the Big Sky Area, site of
the 1973-74 National North American Cross Country Ski

Championship races. The area offers thirty-five miles of first class trails. Hundreds of miles of snowmobile trails are provided by local agencies and by the U.S. Forest Service. Montana has nine national forests, containing nearly sixteen million acres of public land. In addition to offering some of the most challenging snowmobile trails in the West, the forests provide plenty of uncrowded space for touring and primitive camping. Write the U.S. Forest Service, Federal Building, Missoula 59801.

The million-acre Glacier National Park is open through the winter season, December to May. Snowmobiling is permitted on designated trails and touring is allowed at lower elevations. Register at park headquarters. For details, contact the Superintendent, Glacier National Park, West Glacier 59936.

Utah. Write to the Utah Travel Council, Council Hall, Salt Lake City 84114. With forty-three state parks and eight national forests, there is plenty of public land open to all types of winter activities. However, the greatest attraction for the winter camper is found in Utah's five national parks. These parks are open the year-round and provide some of the most spectacular cold-weather camping in the United States. All of the parks display, in multicolored rock, the strangely beautiful work of erosion. Snow, of course, adds a touch of the fantastic to their remarkable, badland beauty. Though not all of the parks receive snowfall, Arches, Zion, and Bryce Canyon generally have snow cover. Bryce Canyon is the favorite of the snowmobilers. The only requirements are that you register and stay on existing roads. Arches and Zion are the parks preferred by winter campers and backpackers. For details, write the Superintendent of: Arches National Park, c/o Canyon Lands National Park, Moab 84532; Bryce Canyon National Park, Utah 84717; Canyon Lands National Park, Moab 84532; Capitol Reef National Park, Torrey 84775; or Zion National Park, Springdale 84767.

Wyoming. Write to the Wyoming Recreation Commission, P.O. Box 309, Cheyenne 82001. Jackson Hole is the center of

Ski touring is popular in Yellowstone National Park, which now stays open year-round. Here Old Faithful spews into the winter sky. (Photo courtesy of the Montana Department of Highways)

winter activity in Wyoming. A small resort town in the northwest corner of the state, it provides private facilities for all types of winter sports. In addition, it offers access to forest areas and to Yellowstone National Park. There are several other ski areas in the state, located in national forests, but provisions for organized camping and facilities for RVers are very limited. However, the five national forests provide unrestricted winter camping and some areas permit snowmobiles. For information on the Bighorn, Medicine Bow, and Shoshone National Forests, write to U.S. Forest Service, Regional Office, Federal Building, Denver, Colorado 80225. For the Bridger and Teton National Forests, write the U.S. Forest Service, Regional Office, Ogden, Utah 84401.

Wyoming's outstanding winter recreation area is the world famous Yellowstone National Park. Its 3,400 square miles offer spectacular scenery, headlined by geysers, hot springs, and mud volcanoes. Wildlife abounds in the park and, during the latter part of the winter, there often are opportunities for dramatic, close-up photos of wild animals. The park remains open during the entire winter season, December through April. Yellowstone provides impressive scenery for the snowshoer and cross country skier. There are several mountain touring trails and snowmobiling is permitted on major roadways. Snow camping is permitted throughout the winter. For information, address the Superintendent, Yellowstone National Park 82190.

THE FAR WEST

California. Write to the California Department of Parks and Recreation, P.O. Box 2390, Sacramento 95811. Cold-weather camping generally is confined to northern California. Yet it includes state and national parks as well as most of the national forests of the state. Camping in state parks during the winter season requires the purchase of off-season or of year-round, day-use permits. Unlike summer camping, no reservations are required and sites are taken on a first-come basis. There are eight national forests in northern California that offer a variety of winter activities. They include Klamath, Lassen, Mendocino, Modoc, Plumas, Shasta-Trinity, Six Rivers, and Tahoe National Forest. For information, write to the U.S. Forest Service, Regional Office, 630 Sansome Street, San Francisco 94111.

Two national parks remain open through the winter season, mid-December to Easter. In both parks, there are maintained touring trails and snowmobiling is permitted on designated roads. Snow camping also is permitted with no specific area requirements. For details, write to the Superintendent of: Lassen Volcanic National Park, Mineral 96063 or Yosemite National Park, P.O. Box 577, Yosemite National Park 95389.

Oregon. Write the Oregon State Highway Division, Travel Information Section, Salem 93710. With 238 state parks, 13

Skiers on a cross-country run in California's Inyo National Forest. (Photo courtesy of the U.S. Forest Service)

national forests, a national park, and Bureau of Land Management recreation areas, there are millions of acres of public land in the state open to all winter activities. Most of the national forests have marked and maintained trails for snowmobilers. Maps are available from forest supervisors or from the regional office. There also are trails for snowshoers, ski tourers, and dog sledders. The most popular areas for ski touring are Mt. Hood, Willamette, Deschutes, Winema, Rogue River, Wallowa-Whitman, and Umatilla National Forests. For

Cross-country ski campers on Oregon's Mt. Hood. (Photo courtesy of the Oregon State Highway Department)

information, write the U.S. Forest Service, Regional Office, 319 SW Pine Street, Portland 97208.

Crater Lake National Park is open during the winter season, December through May. There are trails for snowmobiling and touring. Snow camping is permitted, but registration is required. For details, write the Superintendent, Crater Lake National Park, P.O. Box 7, Crater Lake 97604.

Washington. Write the State of Washington, Department of Natural Resources, Olympia 98504. The Department maintains a road system of nearly 6,000 miles that snowmobilers can use, snow conditions permitting. Marked trails for snowshoeing and ski touring are found in most of the state's six national forests. The favorite areas are Mt. Baker, Snoqualmie, Wenatchee, and Gifford Pinchot National Forests. For details, write the U.S. Forest Service, Regional Office, Box 3623, Portland, Oregon 97208.

There are three national parks in Washington open during the winter season, December through May. All three allow snowmobiling on designated roads and trails. Areas for snowshoeing and touring also are provided. At Mount Rainier National Park snow camping is permitted only at the Sunshine Point Campground. In Cascades and Olympic Parks, snow camping is permitted with no areas designated. For information, write the Superintendent of: Mount Rainier National Park, Longmire 98397; North Cascades National Park, Sedro Woolley 98284; Olympic National Park, 600 East Park Avenue, Port Angeles 98362.

CANADA

Alberta. Write to Travel Alberta, 10255 104 Street, Edmonton, Alberta. There are 150,000 square miles of provincial forest areas, administered by the Alberta Forest Service. In addition, there are fifty-one provincial parks and five national parks in the province. Most of them are open to winter camping. Jasper and Banff National Parks have special provisions for winter campers.

There also are many public and private campgrounds that remain open during the winter season, November through May.

There is plenty of opportunity for snowmobiling, ski touring, and snowshoeing, both supervised and unsupervised. Snowmobiling is not permitted in provincial parks but is allowed in some national parks on designated trails.

British Columbia. Write the Department of Travel Industry, Government of British Columbia, 1019 Wharf Street, Victoria,

Snowmobiling in the Sunshine Area near Banff in Alberta. (Photo courtesy of the Alberta Government Photo Services)

B.C. More than sixty ski areas help keep the roads open for winter campers and offer a jump-off point for touring. In addition, there are 117 provincial campgrounds and four national parks. Not all of them are open to winter camping, but there are enough to provide plenty of snowmobiling, touring, and camping in all areas of the province.

Manitoba. Contact the Department of Tourism and Recreation, 408 Norquay Building, 401 York Avenue, Winnipeg 1, Manitoba. There are ten provincial parks containing

5,000 campsites. Another 5,000 campsites are operated by various public and private groups. Public lands also include seven provincial forests and one national park. Nearly all of these areas provide for snowmobiling, ski touring, and snowshoeing on marked trails. Camping is permitted in campgrounds during the winter, but you are asked to notify the park or forest ranger of your presence. Organized winter camping is offered at Bird's Hill Provincial Park.

In the northern part of the province, a vast expanse of frozen lakes and spruce forests offers limitless possibilities.

New Brunswick. Write to Travel and Tourist Development, 796 Queen Street, Fredericton, N.B. The province of New Brunswick provides extensive facilities for the winter camper. In addition to private facilities, there are three provincial parks and one national park where recreation facilities are available year round. Mactaquac Provincial Park and Fundy National Park maintain special facilities for winter campers. These include cleared campsites, dry toilets, hand pumps, and kitchen shelters stocked with wood. At Mactaquac and near Fundy, there are cleared trailer pads and electrical hookups for the RV camper. All parks provide plenty of trails for snowmobiling, touring and snowshoeing. There also are wilderness areas where more adventurous campers can break their own trails.

The winter season extends from mid-November through mid-March. Though there is an average ninety-two-inch snowfall during the period, daytime temperatures average 33 degrees F. and the sun shines 100 hours a month.

Ontario. Write to the Ministry of Industry and Tourism, 900 Bay Street, Hearst Block Queen's Park, Toronto, Ontario. The Ministry estimates that some 8,000 campers take advantage of the more than 100 provincial parks kept open to handle winter visitors. Arrowhead, Sibbald Point, Pinery, and Rondeau Parks offer winterized campgrounds for visitors. Facilities include cleared roads, cleared campsites, heated washrooms with hot running water, fuel wood, garbage disposal units,

Snowmobile campers set up in the forest near Barrie, Ontario. (Photo courtesy of the Ontario Ministry of Industry and Tourism)

and drinking water. There also are cleared pads and electrical hookups for recreational vehicles. Daily vehicle entry and campsite permits cost $3.50, plus 50 cents for an electrical outlet. A vehicle permit alone costs $1.50 and snowmobile entry is $1.00.

In all other provincial parks, winter camping is permitted free of charge, but interior roads are not cleared. There are vast areas of wilderness here to challenge the hardy.

Quebec. Write the Department of Tourism, Fish and Game, 930 St. Foy Road, Quebec, Quebec. In the provincial parks and forest preserves, miles and miles of trail are provided for snowmobiling, ski touring, and snowshoeing. There is organized winter camping in Mont Tremblant Park. In the Portneuf

Ski tourer travels through the snowy beauty of Quebec's Larentides Park.
(Photo courtesy of the Government of Quebec, Department of Tourism)

Snowmobiling in
Saskatchewan.
(Photo courtesy
of the Saskat-
chewan Govern-
ment)

Reserve and in Saint Maurice Park, winter cabins are provided at a very low rent. For cabin reservations, contact the Central Reservation Office, 150 E. St. Cyrille Boulevard, Place de la Capitale, Quebec City, Quebec.

Saskatchewan. Write to the Department of Tourism and Renewable Resources, Administration Building, Regina, Saskatchewan. There are eighty-six regional parks and approximately forty of these have camping areas, many of which are being used for winter camping. There are also eleven provincial parks and one national park in the province, but the public campgrounds in these parks close in September and snow camping is not prohibited.

Appendix

SUPPLIERS

Alpine Designs, 6185 E. Arapahoe, Boulder, Colo. 80303 (general supplies and equipment)

Bauer, Eddie, P.O. Box 3700, Seattle, Wash. 98124 (general supplies and equipment)

Bean, L. L., Inc., Freeport, Maine 04032 (general supplies and equipment)

Black, Thom, & Sons, 930 Ford St., Ogdensburg, N.Y. 13660 (general supplies and equipment)

Browning, P.O. Box 500, Morgan, Utah 84050 (sleeping bags, down clothing)

Cabela's Inc., 812 13th Ave., Sidney, Nebr. 69162 (general supplies and equipment)

Camp Trails, 4111 West Clarendon Ave., Phoenix, Ariz. 85019 (tents, packs)

Coleman Company, 250 N. St. Francis, Wichita, Kans. 67201 (bags, tents, stoves, refrigerators)

Co-op Wilderness Supply, 1432 University Ave., Berkeley, Calif. 94702 (general supplies and equipment)

Don Gleason's Camper's Supply, Pearl St., Northhampton, Mass. 01060 (tents, packs, bags, accessories)

Eastern Mountain Sports, 1041 Commonwealth Ave., Boston, Mass. 02215 (general supplies and equipment)

Eureka Tent, Inc., 625 Conklin Rd., Binghamton, N.Y. 13902 (tents)

Forrest Mountaineering, Ltd. 5050-M-Fox St., Denver, Colo. 80216 (packs)

Gander Mountain, P.O. Box 248, Wilmot, Wis. 53192 (general supplies and equipment)

Gerry, 5450 N. Valley Hwy., Denver, Colo. 80216 (general supplies and equipment)

Herter's, Route No. 2, Mitchell, S. Dak. 57301 (general supplies and equipment)

Hi-Touring, 1251 East 2100 South, Salt Lake City, Utah 84106 (packs)

Holubar, Box 7, Boulder, Colo. 80302 (general supplies and equipment)

Jansport, Paine Field Industrial Park, Everett, Wash. 98204 (tents, bags, packs)

Kelty, 1801 Victory Blvd., Glendale, Calif. 91201 (general supplies and equipment)

Moor and Mountain, Tracy Rd., Chelmsford, Mass. 01824 (general supplies and equipment)

North Face, P.O. Box 2399, Station A, Berkeley, Calif. 94702 (bags, clothes, tents, accessories)

Primus, 354 Sackett Pt. Road, North Haven, Conn. 06473 (stoves)

Recreation Equipment, Inc., 1525 11th Ave., Seattle, Wash. 98122 (general supplies and equipment)

Ridgeline Industries, Inc., Clayton, N.Y. 13624 (tents)

Sierra Designs, 4th and Addison Sts., Berkeley, Calif. 94703 (tents, packs, clothes, snowshoes)

Ski Hut, 1615 University Ave., Berkeley, Calif. 94703 (general supplies and equipment)

Smilie Co., 575 Howard St., San Francisco, Calif. 94105 (general supplies and equipment)

Stephenson's, 23206 Hatteras St., Woodland Hills, Calif. 91364 (tents, bags)

Survival Systems, Inc., 1830 S. Baker Ave., Ontario, Calif. 91761 (signal flares, etc.)

Thermos Co., Norwich, Conn. 06360 (vacuum bottles, tents, refrigerators)

Three M Company, Public Relations, 135 W. 50th St., New York, N.Y. 10020 (masks)

Turnex, Inc., Box 70, Scotch Plains, N.J. 07076 (masks)

FOODS

Chuck Wagon Foods, Micro Drive, Woburn, Maine 01801

Dri Lite Foods, 11333 Atlantic, Lynwood, Calif. 90262

H & M Packing Corp., 915 Ruperta Ave., Glendale, Calif. 90262

Oregon Freeze Dry Foods, (Teakettle and Mountain House) 770 W. 29th Ave., Albany, Ore. 97321

Perma-Pak, 40 East 2430 South, Salt Lake City, Utah 84115

Rich-Moor Corp., Box 2728, Van Nuys, Calif. 91404

Stow-A-Way Sports Inc., 166 Cushing Hwy., Rt. 3A, Cohasset, Mass. 02025

Trail Chef, P.O. Box 60041 Terminal Annex, Los Angeles, Calif. 90060

Wilson Certified Foods, Inc., 4545 Lincoln Blvd., Oklahoma City, Okla. 73105

GROUP TRIPS AND INSTRUCTION

Mountain Travel, Inc., 1398 Solano Ave., Albany, Calif. 94706

National Hiking and Ski Touring Assn., P.O. Box 7421, Colorado Springs, Colo. 80933

Rocky Mountain Expeditions, Inc., P.O. Box 576, Buena Vista, Colo. 81211

University of the Wilderness, 1325 Delaware St., Denver, Colo. 80204

The Wilderness Society, 1901 Pennsylvania Ave. N.W., Washington, D.C. 20006

OTHER USEFUL ADDRESSES

Burnham Bros., Box 0-124-F, Marble Falls, Tex. 78654 (predator and game calls)

Carikit, Holubar, Box 7, Boulder, Colo. 80302 (sew it yourself bags, packs, tents, down clothing)

Frostline, Dept. 3, 452 Burbank, Broomfield, Colo. 80020 (sew it yourself bags, packs, tents, down clothing)

Hubbard, 2855 Shermer Rd., Northbrook. Ill. 60062 (maps)

Index

223